FOUNDATIONS FOR ORTHO

FOUNDATIONS FOR ORTHODOX CHRISTIAN EDUCATION

JOHN BOOJAMRA

ST. VLADIMIR'S SEMINARY PRESS
CRESTWOOD, NEW YORK 10707
1989

Library of Congress Cataloging-in-Publication Data

Boojamra, John Lawrence.
   Foundations for Orthodox Christian education / John Boojamra.
      p. cm.
   Bibliography: p.
   Includes index.
   ISBN 0-88141-050-0 : $8.95
   1. Christian education--North America. 2. Orthodox Eastern
Church--Education--North America. 3. Christian education--
Philosophy. I. Title.
BX270.B66 1989
268.8197--dc19   89-6075
                                           CIP

FOUNDATIONS FOR ORTHODOX CHRISTIAN EDUCATION

ISBN 0-88141-050-0

PRINTED IN THE UNITED STATES
OF AMERICA
by
J&J Printing, Inc.
Syracuse, New York

Contents

Preface

This book is a joyful offering to the future of Orthodox Christian education in North America. It was written and is published under the assumption that there is such a future available to us in North America, and more generally, in the western world. It is this western matrix, for better or for worse, in which we now find ourselves. Indeed, some of us, as is the case with the author, really know no other world in which to live our Orthodoxy and construct our family life.

This book, in any redeeming feature it may have, does not belong to the author; it more properly belongs to the many friends and colleagues who have made it possible. Any idea which is clearly expressed and is of any practical worth has its root in the many and endless conversations with such friends as Fathers Joseph Allen and Paul Tarazi; it is their Antiochian predispositions which have sharpened the author's sense of his own need to respond to this age and this place as creatively and faithfully as possible. It has been my wife Stellie, who more than most human beings is able to reduce everything to its immediate and essential elements, who has forced me to deal with the reality of "every-day" life. She has taught me the preciousness of "every day" and if the Gospel of what God has done for us in his Son means anything, it means it "at all times and in every place." It is this reality that I hope this book will enable us to perceive and communicate more effectively.

It has been this author's hope that the approach refined and presented in this book will enable pastors, parents, and educators to find the framework for a meaningful response to the North American social and spiritual situation. Nonetheless, the themes developed in this book, I believe, will be universally applicable to Orthodox educational settings in general and to those settings on a variety of levels from the elementary to the graduate theological school.

At this point is is appropriate to express my deepest gratitude to those who have assisted me in my preparation of this book. First, and certainly foremost, is the constant and unfailing support of Metropolitan Philip Saliba, primate of the Antiochian Orthodox Christian Archdiocese. It has been his friendship, sense of urgency, and financial support of my Department of Christian Education which has made the writing of this book possible. My thanks to Eleana Silk, Secretary of the Orthodox Christian Education Commission, who provided practical assistance in the preparation of this manuscript, albeit sustained by many cups of hot chocolate. Finally, my appreciation to my students at St. Vladimir's Seminary who, through their long-suffering patience, and sometimes their impatience, provided me with the feedback to both correct and expand my own thinking on the topics of socialization, family, and moral development. I look forward to the gift of many more years with them.

Dedication

*This book is dedicated to the memory of my wife
Stellie Ann,
whose love, patience, and endurance
daily taught us what courage and
faithfulness to Christ means.*

CHAPTER 1

The Foundations

The Orthodox Churches of North America are formally committed to Christian education. Since at least the late 1940s they have followed the pattern of the Protestants and Roman Catholics and have focused their attention on the education of children according to a school model. This has distorted not only the place of children and the role of the family, but also the nature of the educational process and the Church as educator. This book will explore the thesis that the entire Church is the educator, that each member—the Christian person—is a learner, and that the Church's life in all its aspects is the matrix for the educational ministry. It will argue that what is life-changing is not only belonging to the Church as a community but also the *sense* of that belonging. Inasmuch as the object of the educational ministry is the *person*, we will explore the nature of personhood and the person as a learner. Without this twofold emphasis on the community as teacher and the person as learner, we cannot speak meaningfully of Christian education. Christian education will take place only when the needs of the learner and the needs of the Church are the foundation for determining the content, process, and location of our educational efforts.

Christian education is by its nature total education. It involves total persons throughout their lives, and it involves the total parish in every aspect of its life. It cannot be limited to or defined by the classroom, with the child as the sole learner or the teacher as the sole educator. In attempting to determine fundamentals on which to base a viable approach to a total parish education, I have selected three categories in which to develop my thesis: socialization as a model of Christian belonging, the family as the source of personality characteristics, and morality as a developmental phenomenon. I have tried in each chapter, as in this introduction, to establish an ideological basis in the Fathers and practices of the Church. The Church's tradition and history will be seen to be congenial to the synthesis I am attempting here.

First, however, the stage must be set by noting that we Orthodox have accepted certain presuppositions of the secular school and of Protestant and Roman Catholic education which are counterproductive and have damaged our own tradition. The following five education dysfunctions summarize these foundational misconceptions:

1. We have made children the subject of all educational efforts, and specifically children between the ages of 6 and 16. We have violated learning theory by assuming that children can learn everything without the experience necessary to permit rooting; education is something that adults direct to children and rarely to each other.

2. We have made the classroom and the school the only legitimate places for the educational enterprise and have reduced all other options, including fellowship and liturgical participation to a minimum.

3. If we have identified all learning with the school, we have also identified all teaching with classroom teachers; we have lost the notion of the entire

community—all Christians—as the teacher and have restricted it to certain more or less qualified individuals who are more or less willing each year to undertake the burden of the church school program.

4. We have ignored adults as learners and accepted the relatively common stereotype that adults do not learn much after the age of twenty or at the latest twenty-six. When adult education is conducted, it is treated as just more childhood education and is carried out in the same format. We have ignored the fact that Christianity is religion of adults, presented in adult categories, and speaking to needs that adults, through life-experiences, have come to possess.

5. Because we have focused our attention on children, we have distorted the Church by simplifying it so it can be understood; Christian education has reduced it to facts, dates, numbers and doctrines that can be presented in a classroom in a forty-five minute period.

Each of these dysfunctional distortions of the educational ministry focuses on the place of the person and the community in the educational process. Symptomatic of this are the role and place assigned to children. We have determined that they are the focus of all educational efforts and resources, when in fact they should not be! In the process of centering on children, we offer them a distorted image of the faith and life of the Church; we have for the sake of schooling our children confused the fragile balance between fact and faith in the life of the Church, between explanation and experience, product and process. Education has become something that the Church does to its children, rather than something that happens to them by their interaction with and experience in the Church, the faith, the family, and their own growing and developing selves. Nevertheless, the Church has long known that non-verbal or relational learning is infinitely more significant in Christian education than is verbal or school learning. I by no means wish to suggest that there are not sound religious educators "out there" who already have affirmed what I have and will be saying. Certainly John H. Westerhoff and Iris Cully fall into this category and should be no means be avoided by Orthodox educators.

People, however, learn developmentally throughout their lives, and in many respects learn better as they get older because of motivation and experience. People learn differently at different ages; they learn more efficiently, effectively, and meaningfully as they mature, because all learning is relational and contextual. The Church as a community of persons in communion through and in the Person of Jesus Christ is the context of any genuine Christian nurture and learning. All Christian learning is a process of interaction and growth in understanding from one stage of spiritual development to another. There is little in the history of the Church that allows us to believe that the act of becoming a Christian was ever anything other than a process; conversion was channeled, for instance, through the institution of the catechumenate. It was a controlled and deliberately planned program of moral and spiritual nurture based on an increasing integration in the shared work and worship of the Christian Church. The traditional ecclesiastical pattern of integration was *formational* and not *informational*, the latter of which has become the pattern of Christian education.

That learning is both relational and developmental is the foundation of all modern education. The growth of the human mind and the experience of the human person are equally foundational to genuine learning. Early in this century, John Dewey wrote:

Since the mind is a growth, it passes through a series of stages, and only gradually attains to its majority. That the mind of the child is not identical with the mind of the adult is, of course, no new discovery. After a fashion, everybody has always known it; but for a long, long time the child was treated as if he were only an abbreviated adult; a little man or a little woman. His purposes, interests, and concerns were taken to be about those of the grown-up person, unlikenesses being emphasized only on the side of strength and power.[1]

Learning is conditioned by the cognitive and emotional development of the human mind as well as the experience and the maturity that such development enables. Dewey later wrote:

To attempt to force prematurely upon the child either the mature ideas or the spiritual emotions of the adult is to run the risk of a fundamental danger, that of forestalling future deeper experiences which might otherwise in their season become personal realities to him. We make the child familiar with the form of the soul's great experiences of sin and of reconciliation and peace, of discord and harmony of the individual with the deepest forces of the universe, before there is anything in his own needs or relationships in life which make it possible for him to interpret or realize them.[2]

John Dewey's comments touch on what was also the common experience of the early Church: to push development and learning, it was believed, could hinder the very learning and development intended. In fact, most of us adults carry infantile, distorted notions of God, the Church, and religion—notions based on what we were taught as children before we possessed the maturity to grasp them. How many Orthodox still respond to suffering as a personal punishment from a vengeful God? How many Orthodox still pray to a God who sits on a throne and sports a long white beard? How many still feel, even though they consciously deny it, that God rewards and punishes according to our actions? That our sufferings are somehow related to previous actual or imagined sinful deeds?

In the following chapters, much of my discussion about redirecting the educational enterprise will be along lines supported not only by contemporary educational research, but by the common-sense experience of the Church, and especially the Desert Fathers.[3] As spiritual advisors they knew well the limitations and potential of human nature and the human mind. This realization is surprisingly true of St Gregory of Nazianzus who took up this theme of learning in the *Defense of His Flight to Pontus.*[4] It is as if Gregory had read John Dewey and then went on to critique fourth-century teaching methods. He notes of Scripture study that those who are immature, in their "habit babes,"

> if it were presented to them beyond their strength, they would probably be overwhelmed and oppressed, owing to the inability of their mind...to digest and appropriate what is offered to it, and so would lose even their original power.[5]

And he warns that if you try to overfeed or misfeed students, they will not be strengthened but annoyed.

> And with good reason, for they would not be strengthened according to Christ, nor make that laudable increase, which the word produces in one who is rightly fed, by making him a perfect man, and bringing him to the measure of spiritual stature (Ephesians 4:13).[6]

Hence, the very content of the Church's teachings is understood to be conditioned by age, need, and experience, as well as by the innate deficiency of the subject matter itself.

Gregory describes the chaotic situation in the Church in

which anyone teaches, regardless of preparation in Scripture or for understanding the students. He notes, for instance, that no one is born holy. Implying that Samuel in the Old Testament (1 Samuel 2) was the exception, he warns that teachers and pastors should not fancy themselves like Samuel:

> We are at once wise teachers, of high estimation in Divine Things, the first of scribes and lawyers; we ordain ourselves men of heaven and seek to be called rabbi by men (Matthew 23:7).[7]

He urges instead that we should learn the Scripture and teach each person what is appropriate to his age and maturity. Gregory of Nazianzus writes that, unlike the Hebrews, whose instructional techniques he admired, "there is no boundary line between the giving and receiving of instruction...."[8] He complains that no rules or degrees of presentation are followed. The rule (Hebrews 5:14) is that any difficult passage of Scripture is confined to those whose experience and maturity is a formal guarantee against the abuse of the passage. Teachers, however, settle too easily for hearsay and summaries rather than direct study.

The only way to correct this is to see education as a lifelong process, everyone as student and teacher, and every place as school. We have to stop assuming that children are the only proper objects of education. Childhood is, of course, a foundational period in human development, but we are educating not children but people. Education is about their lifelong transformation, not just about one stage of their lives. I have tried to identify and focus on the non-school aspects of education of some logically consistent way. I would like pastors and educators in the Church to consider the foundations of Christian education, community, Church, family, and the nature of human development in order to avoid the all-too-frequent reliance on the apparent security of the school and the child.[9] The form, however, is as important as the content since it conveys the content. The Church has used many forms, and all we need insist upon is congruency with the content. For total parish education planning we must distinguish between *school* and *education*, and *child* and *learner*.

The early Church always placed learning in the context of the experience of the community as shared work and worship. When many religious educators[10] refer to the restoration of primitive catechesis, including the use of the word, they fail to realize that the catechetical forms and structure of the early Church were almost exclusively adult oriented and experiential. In a real sense the early Church was McLuhanesque[11] in that the medium was itself the message! The values and style of life that the Christian community demonstrated were what commended it to non-Christians. According to the *Catechetical Orations* of St Cyril of Jerusalem, the significance of Baptism and Eucharist could only be realized by experiencing them; he therefore put off teaching about them until after Pascha and the baptism of the catechumens.[12] All educational efforts were directed at adults, as in the catechumenate for instance. Children were left in the hands of their parents, as St John Chrysostom tells us, and their education from their parents was largely occasional and by modeling rather than by formal instruction. In fact, little is said of children, nor was any formal content directed at children in what was several hundred years of educational history highlighted by such teachers as Augustine, St Cyril of Jerusalem, St John Chrysostom, Origen, and Clement of Alexandria, all noted teachers with more or less defined curricula for new believers.[13] What is clear is that membership in the Church was accompanied by the shared work and worship of the community. It is this latter realization from the history of the catechumenate, for instance, that has forced me to use developmental theories and a socialization model as the basis of Christian education and nurture.

This emphasis on the multidimensional integration into the actual community of faith, which I refer to here as the socialization process, was transformed historically by the Reformation and the printed word. Up until the sixteenth century, learning was largely oral, experiential, and adult oriented. Its success or failure did not depend on material but on parents, priests, and the Christians with whom the learner came into contact. The printing press standardized the communication of the faith. It is, for instance, not by accident that the sixteenth century, that of the Reformation is also the century of schools, creeds, and confessions, when statements of beliefs became primary. The stuff of the Church became identified with content, to the exclusion of the person and the relationship between person, content, and teacher. Content was formalized and crystallized by the onset of the printed word, called the "Guttenberg Galaxy" by Marshal McLuhan, which came to fruition in Luther. We are all children of Luther's passion for the written word as well as his belief that the faithful must be permitted, enabled, and required to read the Bible. The development of religious education as a formal school enterprise has been so tied with publication and the written word that we cannot escape the compulsion of the "book." Along with a passion for the written word came the necessity of the teacher and the classroom as isolated entities, operating as independent agencies apart from the Church. The schooling-instructional paradigm necessitated an *informational* approach to Christian education. We ignore the point completely that the process and context are far more essential than the material, especially in adult and adolescent education.

In the 1950's Marshal McLuhan pointed out the serious

limitations of the so-called Guttenberg Galaxy and its reliance on the text and the written word as opposed to the experience. His now common expression "the medium is the message"[14] had in fact been the Church's experience since it took breath from the Spirit of God at Pentecost. It is in this context that I believe we must return to the more historical socialization model for Christian education. As John H. Westerhoff III has pointed out, the schooling model has failed to "make" Christians because it was never equipped to make Christians.[15] The socialization model, which I develop in chapter 2, offers a picture of learning as an encounter with a living community, the Church, and the Lord of that community, Jesus Christ. To be faithful to this distinction between product and process we must define the relationship between the affective and the cognitive approach to learning. The Eastern approach, as McLuhan has already shown with reference to the Far East, but with application to the Orthodox East, is the emphasis on the primacy—both logical and chronological—of the experience. First I do, and then I learn about what I did! The ongoing controversy in the U.S. between the content and experience-centered curricula is but one expression of this ongoing search for a starting point.

I believe, along with many Roman Catholic educators, that Christian education is neither preaching nor catechesis.[16] In fact, Christian education is education like any other education, using the same mental faculties as any other.[17] Religious education describes a different though complementary process from catechesis and preaching since it is more actively concerned with discussing, questioning, digesting, dissecting, and reflecting—activities not appropriate to a preaching situation. Preaching depends on a personal response, but teaching *enables* a personal response. In teaching, change is sought by process and not by proclamation (a product-oriented approach). Teaching aims at developing meaning since meaning cannot be transmitted by preaching or catechesis unless a response can be stimulated; meaning is the hearer's/learner's gift to the process. Meaning cannot be given. We can only enable meaning or remove barriers to meaning.[18] In spite of the necessary distinction I perceive between teaching and preaching, both must be underwritten by theology and both must be informed by the life of the Church; otherwise, there is no living context in which meaning can be worked out.[19]

The Church as educator has been ignored largely due to the several periods and episodes of captivity when it could not assume a formal format. More recently, the role has been given only slight attention theologically because, in the minds of Protestants and Roman Catholics and certainly Orthodox, it tends to be associated with the secular education movement rather than with the Church itself—which had traditionally taken refuge in its liturgical functions and relegated education and social service to the realm of the secular. Education, and specifically total parish education, has its roots in the tradition of the Church. We must affirm these roots. The priest is a preacher and a celebrator, but he is also an educator. It is the role of the priest as educator that has received scant attention in the curricula of our theological seminaries.

People are dynamic organisms constantly growing or dying, but never remaining static. The nature of the person is to change—a reality that offers both difficulties and opportunities for pastors, parents, and teachers. We can even describe statistically what people are doing, are supposed to be doing, or how they are changing at certain ages and stages. Contemporary developmental psychologists such as Jean Piaget, Erik Erikson, and Lawrence Kohlberg have described the developing human person from birth through old age as a learning and changing, assimilating and accommodating organism, growing emotionally, cognitively, and morally toward adequacy. Their research and conclusions have informed much of this work and will be seen to be of assistance to the nascent Christian education community in the Orthodox Churches of North America.

Nor is the evangelical message static; it is rooted in the dynamism of God's search for people and their active response. The pattern for patristic understanding of personhood is *synergeia* or divine-human cooperation, literally, "joint work," for salvation. Similarly, the communication of meaning is a joint endeavor achieved only when the teacher acts as guide, helping the learner to organize his experiences *meaningfully*. Meaning lies within the individual and not in the material; it must be derived. The teachers facilitates this by the logical organization of material.[20] Again, nowhere do we find this *response* presented in the writings of the Fathers, and most especially the Desert Fathers,[21] as a static, once-and-for-all "born again" phenomenon. Perhaps the best metaphor we can use as Orthodox is not that of product, but of process and pilgrimage: Christian education, as a curriculum, is the route over which we travel under the leadership of an experienced guide and companion, and in the community of the faithful. It is not a once-and-for-all given, extrinsic to human participation.

Each particular stage of life offers opportunities—for what the person is able to learn and what the person needs to learn. One of the first principles of Christian education is the realization, common to the monastic communities, that people are both the same and different, and both aspects must be explored in formulating programs, producing materials and organizing learning situations. The learner's possibilities for participating and responding are unbounded. Nor are curriculum planners bound by a fixed content; any aspect of the Church's life can be taught as typical of the whole, depending on the people with whom we are working.[22] This, however, means selecting those aspects of the Church's life that suit the people and, at the same time, are faithful to the *given* of the Church. This is not pandering to the whims of the people and betraying the Gospel; it is taking personhood, process, and community seriously. A child of six does not have the ability to understand the content of the Christian message to the same degree as a teenager, who in turn does not have the same ability to understand as an adult. Popular works such as *Passages*[23] by Gail Sheehey and the more technical works by developmentalists such as Piaget and Erikson outline the needs of people at different ages, which can be used as the basis for teaching the Gospel message. It is their work as well as our own common sense observations that enable us to ask such questions as: What needs do people in their 30's have? people in their 40's? in their 50's? One thing seems to be certain: education must begin where people are and bring them to where the Church feels they should be.

The Church also has its needs and makes its demands on the educational process. How do we bring the Church's need to be *the Church* in touch with the needs, interests, and developmental levels of the learners? This is precisely the challenge. The solution, however, is a *local* solution; it falls on the pastor and the people of the local community to plan a total education program for its own learning needs. What becomes significant in the planning process is neither the content, whose emphasis can differ from time to time, nor the people, who also differ from time to time, but the methods we choose to bring together a particular group of Christians and a particular aspect of the Church's life. The planner needs to grasp the fundamentals of people and faith to bring the two together in a meaningful learning process.

Any education program must encourage people, from

their earliest to their latest years, into a deeper and fuller life with Christ in His Church. I emphasize the Church because the Church is the matrix in which we live and grow. There is no such reality as Christianity-at-large or a Christian alone; such a "Christianity" is a deception. There is no Christian education which is not at the same time Church education,[24] education which deepens the person's experiences of the Christian community and the Lord of that community. Christian education is an ecclesiological phenomenon. Both the teacher and the learner are members of the Church and both share the same sacraments and life. The teacher, moreover, is obliged to pass on the faith of the Church, the *paradosis*, not his opinion. While the learner's appropriation of the tradition is always personal, it allows him to share in a community which is at once extended in time and space. Just as there is no Christianity without the Church, so there is no Christian education without a Church focus.

In any educational ministry, regardless of who the object of the ministry is, the Church must in some way be the control, though not necessarily the content, of the program. There has been debate for years on the proper focus of a Christian education curriculum. Among Protestants, the conflict has been between Bible and child-centered programs; among Roman Catholics, between data-centered and life-centered programs; and among Orthodox between life-centered and liturgy-centered programs. The conflict exists only because we as well as the Protestants have a weak notion of the Church. The absence of a clear, working definition of the Church has allowed the many parts of Christian education to hang separately rather than be integrated into an overall living community and fellowship. Each possible focus for education belongs to the Church because the Church is the institution that educates and determines the criteria for experiencing the message in a unique historical expression. The child, for instance, is not isolated, not a Christian alone; he is a child in the Church, a child of the Church, who is to be fed and nurtured so that he can grow into a mature Christian. It is in the context of the Church that the various conflicts related to growth are resolved in a living community of faith.

It is this lack of a definition that has permitted, even encouraged, the separation of the church school from the Church, Christian education from adults, and adults from the Church. We have never placed Christian education on a theological footing or, for that matter, on an ecclesiological footing. Today we focus our educational efforts on the secular format and isolate our children within it. If we define the Church as the matrix in which we can experience what we are teaching, we then provide a foundation to Christian education; we remove the abstraction based on a generalized effort to communicate "Christianity"; and we give something besides abstract ideas and ideals, "disincarnated." When we focus on the structure of the Church and the history of the Church, as well as on participation in the shared work and worship of the Church, then the learner experiences its fellowship. Children, isolated in a church school program, have no place in the Church and so cannot believe that they are the Church. If Christianity is treated as an exotic ideal, somewhere distant, isolated from the parish community, then learners become holders of a faith in a Christianity purer than that of the actual Church itself, and by perverse definition, "superior." Roots in the Church can be built only by a step-by-step participation in the life of the Church as well as by an increasing understanding of what that Church is. In a real sense Christian education is always the follower and can never be said to be the leader of the Church.

The whole Church educates. Not only is every person the

object of the Church's educational efforts, but every member of the Church is the subject of the Church's educational effort. The whole Church educates in all of her life. The greatest error we can make is to identify education with children and school.

What the teacher does in the classroom when he refers to Christian beliefs or to the Church has no meaning apart from what the students experience around them. It is folly to believe that we have no responsibility for educating children because we have no formal teaching status. Certainly one of the greatest barriers to Christian learning, especially to young people and children, is the failure of adult Christians to take the whole enterprise seriously. The image of the adult Christian is formed in the child's mind by what he sees and hears adults doing. It is not uncommon for the child, as soon as he considers himself "grown-up," to drop out, because that is what adults do. Likewise, it is an utter mistake to believe that we have nothing to learn because of our age. All of us are growing, and Christian growth is relational; it happens in the matrix of a community. All of our efforts at Christian education, child or adult, are doomed to failure unless the Church manifests to some degree what is being talked about; because that is all we can do—talk about something. The actual growth comes from within us and the community.

The Orthodox Church has produced no real programming beyond the childhood years because it does not know what to do beyond the written word, the least influential means of instruction. We have conveniently separated the people from learning by giving them no part in the process and proceeded to teach them by one of two methods: either we give them books to read or we lecture to them. These are the easiest approaches, requiring the minimum investment in time, effort, and money. The real problem is that it also requires a minimum investment by the learner, and without investment there is no learning. Developing open-ended materials suitable for teens and adults is difficult because there are a great many variables to account for; there is a failure to understand what they need and how they grow and a failure to attract people or produce people who know how to work with the flexibility required among adults and those becoming adults.

Learning can be as varied as the people being taught and the content being communicated, but certain material is best communicated through certain methods. A series on social involvement, for example, is best done by programming for actual involvement. Variety and open-endedness are the operative words for working with adults. Books and other materials such as video cassettes, movies, and plays are available to stimulate discussion. Schedules can be arranged for any time that you can get a group of people together; the location can be anywhere you need to be. The subject matter can be whatever they are interested in—the Scriptures, the Church, history, liturgy, present-day problems, prayer, fasting, or focal-point events (Pascha, Christmas, death, marriage, and so forth). The focus of any program, of any content, or any format is three-fold—God, people, and method (ἡ Τέχνη). The matrix is always the Church as the "faithing" community.

Fellowship is being with other people who share our faith and our life in the same time and the same place; this also includes fuller fellowship with the saints in the fellowship of God. None of us, especially children, grow in isolation from the rest of the community. Rather, it is in the midst of the caring community that we each take our validation. Religion is not a private matter, even though Americans tend to treat it that way. The illness of twentieth-century North American culture, and western culture in general, is alienation. Ideally, there is no alienation in the Church. Practically speaking, however, local church communities are often as alienated as any other community. The Church provides us, and especially the adolescents among us, with plausible structures and validation for our belief systems as well as our personhood.

One thing is clear: Christianity is a social and relational religion, focusing on community and person in relationship to God. Without others we cannot be Christians, and good fellowship must be the companion of any education program— as well as the object of any education program. It is this emphasis on community and fellowship that logically and eventually gives rise to the inescapable category of *service to the world.*

We must not permit ourselves to be cut off from all that is good, true, and beautiful outside of the Church, simply because it is *outside.* For too long, too many people have been covering up our obvious sloppiness, poor teaching, and poor materials with the excuse made half-lamely that the Holy Spirit will make up the difference. Nonsense! Not that the Holy Spirit could not, but why should He make up the difference or fill in for our willful sloppiness? We are all in a "holding" operation, taking stabs in the dark at everything from creative activities to selecting movies, choosing teachers, arranging lessons. There is much to be learned from secular education; much effort, however, must be made to apply it meaningfully to church education.

First, we need foundations from which we can derive a perspective of the learner, the materials, and the learning process. I have tried to put together here working models of human learning rooted in personhood, the Church, and the family; I have stepped into the muddy waters of moral development as an application of developmentalism conditioned by the experience within the Church and the family. I have tried to focus also on learning theory as a means of enabling us to make contact between the needs of the Church and the needs of the human person, without turning Christian education into anthropology.

Success in formulating workable Christian education programs will not be accidental, neither will it be left to the Holy Spirit alone to clear up our deficiencies, to make everything all right again "as it was in the beginning." It was never "all right," and each Christian age must build its programs, methods, and materials on the foundation of Christian education—the person of Jesus Christ and the community that He has called into existence.

Chapter 1 Footnotes

[1]Iris Cully, *Children in the Church* (Philadelphia: Westminster Press, 1960).

[1A]John Dewey, "Religious Education as Conditioned by Modern Psychology and Pedagogy," *Religious Education*, LIX (January-February, 1974), 6; reprinted from the proceedings of the First Annual Convention of the Religious Education Association, February 10-11, 1903, 60-66.

[2]*Ibid.*, 6-7.

[3]Helen Waddell, *The Desert Fathers* (Ann Arbor, MI: University of Michigan Press, 1960), 59-155.

[4]Gregory Nazianzen, *Defense of His Flight to Pontus* in *Nicene and Post-Nicene Fathers,* series, 2 Vol. VII (Grand Rapids, MI: Eerdmans Publishing Co., 1974), ch 48, 214-215.

[5]*Ibid.*, 214.

[6]*Ibid.*

[7]*Ibid.*, 215.

[8]*Ibid.*, 215.

[9]Gabriel Moran, "From Theory to Practice," *Religious Education*, LXXVII (July-August, 1982), 396. Moran warns of the danger of "psychological reductionism, especially in the use of developmental theories." This is, indeed, a danger if we consider developmental theories as *prescriptive* rather than *descriptive*.

[10]Thomas Groome, "Christian Education for Freedom: A 'Shared-Praxis' Approach," in Padraic O'Hare (ed.), *Foundations of Religious Education*, (New York: Paulist Press, 1978) 8-39, at 14-15.

[11]Marshall McLuhan, *Understanding Media* (New York: McGraw Hill Co, 1964), 7-14.

[12]Cyril of Jerusalem, *Catechetical Orations*, in *Nicene and Post-Nicene Father* series, Vol. VII (Grand Rapids, MI: Eerdmans Publishing Co, 1974), 144.

[13]See for a discussion of these writers, Glanville Downey, "Teacher and Pupil in the Early Church," RISK, II (First Quarter, 1966), 46-51.

[14]McLuhan, *op.cit.*, 7-8.

[15]John H. Westerhoff, III, *Will Our Children Have Faith?* (New York: Seabury Press, 1976), 3:5.

[16]Jacques Audinet, "Catechesis," in K. Rahner (ed.), *Encyclopedia of Theology* (New York: Seabury Press, 1975), 173-178.

[17]Padraic O'Hare, "Religious Education: Neo-Orthodox Influence and Empirical Corrective," *Religious Education*, LXXIII (November-December, 1978), 627-639, at 632.

[18]George Mouly, *Psychology for Effective Teaching* (New York: Holt, Rinehart, and Winston, 1962), 327.

[19]Randolph Crump Miller, *The Clue to Christian Education* (New York: C. Scribner's Sons, 1950), 6, 15.

[20]Mouley, *op.cit.*, 326-327.

[21]*Ibid.*, 326-335.

[22]Philip Phenix, *Realms of Meaning* (New York: McGraw Hill, 1964), 44

[23]Gail Sheehey, *Passages: Predictable Crises of Adult Life* (New York: Bantam Books, 1977.)

[24]James D. Smart. *The Teaching Ministry of the Church,* (Philadelphia, PA: Westminster Press, 1954), 108-116.

CHAPTER 2

Socialization: The Foundation of Christian Integration

With this chapter let us begin to discuss possible alternatives to the "academic-schooling" model we have thus far discussed. A "socialization" model of Christian education is, I think, more appropriate to the needs, theology, and tradition of the Orthodox Church, being congenial both to the nature of human development and to the nature and history of the Orthodox Church. It is a model congenial to our faith and history because it allows for growth in the Christian life as a process rather than for the "manufacturing" of the Christian believer as a product; it speaks about children and adults growing in faith by *living* the faith-life of the Church within a faith-filled local community.

What is clear to anyone in Christian education is that the so-called schooling model has not been effective and in many cases has been counterproductive, deceptive in giving the appearance that something is better than nothing. The Sunday school may indeed have a future, but only if we place it in the broader context of a cross-generational and total parish education effort that is consistent with what has characterized Orthodox community life, that is, a life that is at once both vertical and horizontal. This socialization model can provide us with the framework for planning and renewing parish life. Let us be perfectly clear: the rejection of the schooling-instructional paradigm and the reaffirmation of the liturgical model is not the solution to our education problem. The "liturgical captivity" which has characterized much of our educational materials has in fact distorted both the nature of the Church and Christian education. The Church is, certainly, liturgy, but it is more than liturgy. It is multidimensional and many aspects can more or less adequately express its fullness; there are other aspects of the Church's life—ethical, prayerful, intellectual—which contribute to the ecclesiastical reality which we claim to experience as the Church of God. The job of the learner and the teacher is to come to experience this living Church in all its fullness as relevant and meaningful. For this we will have to move beyond the limited focus of the liturgy or the classroom as exclusive. Toward this goal the following reflections are offered—reflections that take seriously the Church, its history, life and faith, as well as the people with their needs and modes of learning. Although socialization terminology may ring strange in the ears of many Orthodox, it, in fact, reflects what the Church has been doing for centuries in the process of integrating and shaping members for a life of faith lived toward God and toward their brothers and sisters.

Although I do not argue the full case for the propriety of this socialization model, I will provide a basis for further discussions among educators and theologians about the nature of learning in general and the nature of Christian learning in particular. Without this discussion of the context and structure of learning and teaching, we will be unable to plan for effective Christian nurture for all members of the parish.

First, my conclusions: people, both children and adults,

become Christians not by learning *about* Christianity but by being integrated into an existing Church through experiencing the rites, symbols, and stories of the community. In the sense of *integration into* the Church the current sociological model of *socialization* is both convenient and adequate for this discussion. But any model, including a theological one, is never locked into itself or exhaustive of the truth; rather, it hedges in the truth and sets the parameters for understanding what we experience. Models are tools, and like tools can be altered or discarded. I have attempted here to choose a model that would allow for a meaningful discussion of the manner in which the Church has encouraged "faithful" membership.

Theosis, divinization of the person, should be the primary goal of any educational process and material that we devise. The Orthodox Fathers felt deeply the impact of St Peter's words that we are to "become partakers of the divine nature" (2 Peter 1:4). They stressed that becoming a Christian was never a one-shot deal but a process, with baptism as a beginning and not as an end, and a process occurring in community and never in isolation. Part of our job as Christian parents, priests, and educators is to help the baptized person become conscious of what the Holy Spirit has started in him. We are not working with *tabulae rasae*, but with people who possess "histories" in the Church as well as ongoing spiritual lives.

Formal classroom education is certainly one way of encouraging an awareness of this spiritual "history" as the person grows in cognitive ability. This schooling model has, in fact, been the primary emphasis of the western churches since the Protestant and the Tridentine reformations. Schools were the hallmark of the sixteenth century and were, in fact, the earliest substantial, formal childhood education in Christianity.[1] The subsequent emphasis on young children has tended to dull the awareness that Christian nurture is a process and adults are valid objects of an educational ministry. This has led to the unavoidable, albeit mistaken, conclusion that once children grow up, beyond "school" age, they no longer need such a ministry.

The identification of Christian education with the classroom or the academic-schooling paradigm had the effect of identifying Christian education not only with children but with the accumulation of information about the Church and correct doctrine, which was received from adults as from "authorities." Such an arrangement is by its very nature heteronomous—that is, Christian education here is something that adults do to children to help them stop being children. Implicitly, the validity of their childhood is, in sound Puritan style, rejected.[2]

In addition, the academic-schooling paradigm tended to ignore the essence of the community in Orthodox life. No one is a Christian alone! This is quite clear in the Fathers and especially in St Basil the Great, the master of social mutuality, whose ascetical injunctions apply to communities, whether parochial, connubial, or monastic. The goal of life in the community is to allow the growth of "complete Christians" (οἱ τέλειοι Χριστιανοί).[3] In his commentary on Psalm 28 he notes: "Such are the leaders of the disciples of Christ. They *lead* them forth to...nourishment of doctrine, *water* them with living water...raise them up and they *nurture* them until they produce fruit; then they guide them to rest and safety."[4] For Basil, this Christian perfection is a process, never a product. It is not individual, but grows only in community with God and with neighbor. This was the closest any Church Father came to a model for Christian education—although the educational reality may have been there, the vocabulary was not.

The informational approach to learning served a specific

purpose—to make Catholics and Protestants in the polemical context of the mid-sixteenth century. We must reappraise our use of this approach, as it is foreign to the Orthodox Church, which has, in an unwritten format, tended toward a *formational* rather than an *informational* paradigm for learning. It was precisely this *formation* that described the process of integration into a living community, the Church of God, with full membership and cross-generational interaction as one of its hallmarks. This was accomplished primarily through liturgy, but never liturgy in isolation from the rest of life and the rest of church life as *martyria* (witness) and *diakonia* (service).

The term "socialization," as already stated, describes what has always been the Church's pattern of integrating new members as well as nurturing old members. Berard Marthaler, a Roman Catholic, presents it in its most scientific treatment.[5] John H. Westerhoff III, one of the leading contemporary spokesmen for this model, in his *Will Our Children Have Faith*, develops the anthropological notion of faith-enculturation and urges a Protestant return to liturgy, worship and dynamic symbols as the chief means of bringing children to Christian maturity, focusing on life crises. He criticizes what he refers to as the "schooling-instruction" paradigm as counterproductive, inadequate and a distortion of Christian nurture. However, he opts for the anthropological "enculturation" model rather than the socialization model, interpreting enculturation as a process of mutual and cross-generational interaction.[6] Nevertheless, there is no essential difference between enculturation and socialization—any process involving children and adults in an institutional setting involves an inequality by sheer effect of size. Socialization as a term and as a category is quite adequate to the Church's experience, implying as it does in educational terms group-centered or group-directed activity, as opposed to individualized activity.[7] However, one of the weaknesses of socialization theory in Christian education is its emphasis on the *individual* and *collective* rather than the *personal* and *communal.*

Westerhoff affirms (or reaffirms) a worship-centered community life as an alternative to a bankrupt schooling-instructional model. Although he does offer us the ideal of the total integration of the child, he does not, however, go far enough—he calls for an age-focused liturgical life and ignores full infant membership. The child is not a full member since he is not admitted to communion without prior "intellectual assent."[8] What Westerhoff actually refers to is total participation in all activities and a liturgical life readjusted to commemorate marker or crisis events as focuses of "educational" efforts.[9] More recently, and especially in the context of the work of Kohlberg and Samuel Simon in moral development and values clarification, Westerhoff has begun to take on a broader perspective than an essentially liturgical-socialization model. He is currently warning educators not to rely too heavily on nurture at the expense of "evangelization" and the concrete teaching of faith as information. (This will be more evident in the approach to moral development in the last chapter in this book.)

The Orthodox doxological and liturgical approach to Christian life has been well noted by the non-Orthodox, among whom we have become the liturgical "specialists." A liturgical thrust is the heart of this socialization paradigm, and inasmuch as it represents true community action (λεί τουργία) it may in fact be the leading element. Too often, however, an exclusively liturgical model has been offered as the Orthodox paradigm par excellence. Not only has this affirmation often existed more in the breach, but in principle it represents a fragmented approach to total Christian living. In actuality, the liturgy has been emphasized to the exclusion of other historically prominent aspects of Church life.[10] *Leitourgia* is more than προσκύνησις; it is also *diakonia* and *martyria*. It is this which we have apparently forgotten.

In order to draw some conclusions about its suitability for meeting the needs of the Church and the children and its effectiveness in permitting the integration of the child and adult into the life of the Church, let us look briefly at the dialectics of the socialization process and the role of symbols. Socialization is, as I have already pointed out, suitable to our theology because it is a process and not a product-oriented approach, and as such involves the individual in a dialectic with the community and its faith symbols. According to P.L. Berger and Thomas Luckman,[11] the dynamic of the dialectic involves three movements: (1) externalization; (2) objectification; and (3) internalization.

(1) In order to be human, a person must be open to the world outside of himself; he must overcome infantile egocentrism and try to change the world to meet what he perceives as his needs. Social and ecclesiastical structures come into existence to meet this natural need to externalize internal perceptions of spiritual reality.

(2) People create symbols and structures to define what they have experienced and to share these experiences with others. The symbolic structures that persons or communities create exist apart from the persons or the community; the two are never automatically one. The building exists apart from the builder, yet embodies something of the builder. The ecclesiastical symbols are objectifications of the relationship of the people of God with their Lord, but exist apart from that relationship.

(3) *Internalization* describes the reassimilation of this objectified world of meaning into the consciousness. It occurs in such a way that the structure of the Church's

symbol system comes to determine the subjective consciousness of the person himself.[12] Symbols at this stage can shape the people relating to them even if they did not themselves create those symbols.

Socialization is the process whereby the symbol and the person interact. The process of this interaction gives rise to enhanced self-awareness and to awareness of the self as Orthodox. Through systematic interaction in the community, home, or parish with the symbol system and practices of the Church, the child comes to perceive himself as a member of the Orthodox Church. Only to the extent that he internalizes the values, attitudes, behavioral expectations, and symbols of the Church can he come to believe as a member of the Church and be considered a member of the Church. In this sense, perception is extremely important: we can expect Christian behavior and beliefs from a person only to the extent that he comes to perceive himself as a Christian, and symbols play the initial role in shaping such a perception. The basic definition of socialization, then, is the interaction of the individual person with a community and its symbols, which describe and often define that community. Socialization, which connotes a sharing of common meaning and the symbols which express those meanings, permits the development of a sense of belonging, self-identity, and world maintenance (projected stability).

From a peculiarly Christian and Orthodox perspective, we affirm that people are psychosomatic unities. The Church has always affirmed that people do not live exclusively in one realm of life experience but that the total person—body, soul, and mind—shares in theosis. In addition, by virtue of the senses and the body, people can come to a knowledge of God through their total being. It is a theological as well as a psychological principle that a person cannot live in one dimension of reality and continue to be human.[13] In fact, sense experiences are absolutely essential for an adult's emotional well-being and satisfaction. Human touch, for example, is the matrix of our spiritual, social, and emotional relationships with others.

There is in Biblical and patristic morality a mutual interaction between behavior and feeling. Kissing icons, consuming the Eucharist, lifting the hands, bowing the head, processing, carrying candles—all of these actions both result from and influence a person's affective and cognitive domains. In general, the Orthodox have balanced their adoption of the academic-schooling model of Christian education with at least a perfunctory affirmation of liturgical life. This affirmation must be expanded and more intimately associated with the other evangelical virtues; the affective domain must be stimulated and satisfied by liturgy, prayer, service, fasting, etc. This calls not only for a "total person" approach to education, but a "total parish" approach—such is the Biblical and patristic vision of the mutuality of behavior and feeling. And such is the direction offered by a socialization model, in which the physical and the emotional, the behavioral and the passional, have a mutual relationship, providing a wide variety of experiences involving the whole person—touching hearing, tasting, smelling, seeing, feeling.[14] Unlike the exclusively artistic or esthetic, Christian symbols are not arbitrary or merely decorative—rather they reflect the substance of the Church's faith and the content of her experience of her Lord. In this sense, we can say that *certain* art forms are not only *historically* peculiar to the Orthodox Church. Relating to these symbols is normative for the Orthodox believer. For instance, no person can be Orthodox while either rejecting or abstaining from the Holy Eucharist. Without Christian symbols, there is no Christian education, no nurture, and there is no *membership* in the Church. How can there be a Church, a community of the *incarnate Lord*, without a physical expression that carries the message of that incarnation?

By way of contrast, let us look at Protestant development. The Orthodox Church has affirmed the essential goodness, though practical ambivalence, of creation. To this end, the Church, through medieval times, struggled to affirm the validity of representational art. The West had a somewhat less critical development and never quite understood what was happening as the Christians in the East fought over icons.

Historically, evangelical and conservative Protestantism has given art a low priority. The reformers' concerns were a bold contrast to the Roman Catholic cultic and pietistic excesses that had increased since the Renaissance, placing more stress on the externals—paintings, vestments, relics, good works, etc. With their emphasis on the centrality of the grace of God and on preaching the word, the reformers represented only one side of a theological coin, the side which had been inherent since Augustine and which had become more pronounced since the fourteenth century, when the Franciscan William of Occam separated God's actions from man's actions. Luther and the reformers merely accentuated one aspect of a twofold tradition in the western Christian approach, emphasizing God and his grace while rejecting human efforts and arts. There is no sense of *synergy*, as in patristic theology. Calvin's Geneva was noted not only for its sobriety but also for its sterility and absence of symbols. This went to the extreme in some Swiss churches, where the center aisles were actually removed to de-emphasize the symbolism of the Eucharist. The "word" became the chief art form, and Protestant literature has done well by it. Schools proliferated, and education became to a great extent the conveying of information rather than the formation of people through growth into a community through its rites, symbols, and stories.[15] The same was true of pockets in the post-Tridentine Roman Church where schools were set up for street children in Italian towns, for instance.[16]

The deep distrust of art continued in American Puritanism, where simplicity of style, dress, housing, and life became the hallmark. The Puritans built functional structures for churches—not places of mystery or glory but austere places of learning. In addition, they considered their children miniature adults, to be treated as such and shaped by harsh discipline and rote memorization. Clearly, childhood is something relatively new to human history after the Renaissance.[17]

But now the Puritan theological tradition, viewed in the light of contemporary educational theory and psychology, seems inadequate to wholesome development and effective learning.[18] Many American Protestants are calling for a reappraisal of the role of art and liturgy, as well as play.[19] Significantly, the call is coming from among Christian educators. Frank Nelson, for example, "associates it with a rediscovery of the biblical christology and incarnation."[20]

Christian Initiation

By way of apologia for this socialization model of education, let us consider the nature of Christian initiation. The question is not "how does a person become a member of the Church through baptism?" but rather "what is the process whereby a person comes to identify with the Church and be identified as an Orthodox Christian after his baptism?" Baptism is the beginning of a moral and spiritual process of growth and nurture into a community of believers—the Church—that has as its Lord Jesus Christ.

It is significant that the primatial catechumenate for adults was not merely a period of instruction but a period of integration, of sharing limited, yet authentic, aspects of the

Church's life.[21] A limited liturgical integration, by which the person became sensitized to the rituals and symbols of the Church, culminated in the exposition of the *traditio symboli* and the baptismal event. Initiation as an *informational* process came at the end of the catechumenate. As in the case of Cyril of Jerusalem and Ambrose of Milan, for instance, the actual teaching about holy communion and baptism often came later.[22] The socialization model fairly accurately describes what the Church has done in the past and what it must cultivate in the future. Christian life, full Christian life, begins with baptism, confirmation and the immediate reception of holy communion. This threefold movement is, in fact, a profound affirmation of the socialization model. There is no partial membership, only full membership in the Church.

Developmentalism

Religious educators, Orthodox and non-Orthodox alike, are currently fascinated with developmental psychology and its cognitive and affective implications for Christian learning. Adults and parents interested in Christian education in its informational aspects are warned by research in developmental psychology of the inappropriateness, even irrelevance, to young children until about the age of thirteen of doctrinal formulations.

The findings of developmental psychologists—Piaget in the cognitive field, Erikson in the emotional, and Kohlberg in the moral—are, in my opinion, valid, albeit limited in their scope and focus. All we can ask of any "scientific" investigation, including the theological enterprise, is that it realize its limits and the limits of its applications. Basically, the developmentalists have limited their research to the cognitive domain, even in the area of moral development, where the question of Kohlberg is not the content of moral thinking but the structure of such thinking. Piaget, the deceased doyen of developmentalists, would in fact have held that cognitive learning is the main form of learning and is radically distinguishable from the affective. Kohlberg, in the moral realm, does not go so far, but affirms that though they are inseparable they are quite distinguishable. Even though the work of Piaget and Kohlberg represents strong Kantian and Cartesian tendencies toward rationalism and formalism, and the work of Goldman in religious development represents strong Bultmannian demythologizing,[23] their findings are radically sobering for Christian adults, especially pastors and parents. The very limitations of learning ability that they *describe* are also an opportunity we should not miss, for the findings, if valid, would provide the foundation for an enhanced emphasis on the socialization process, where genuine learning can take place through the normal and natural faculties of the child and his relationships. They in fact highlight for us Orthodox the limits of a cognitive approach and represent an implicit criticism of the Reformation and Tridentine emphasis on the academic-schooling model for religious education, which we in North America have adopted so unquestioningly. Piaget's research is supposed to have put to death the Puritan notion of the child as a miniature adult.[25]

The relationship between the person and the Church is not and can never be static. Essentially, without considering moral development or degeneration, the child or, more appropriately, the person grows both through natural impulses and through moral and intellectual guidance. A child, for instance, comes to perceive who he is not epigenetically, but intellectually and socially. No one is automatically Orthodox because he is raised as such; we can never lose sight of the need for effective education and evangelization. The child must be told who he is, who he is to become, and, more importantly, who God is. Just as in moral development, personality development cannot ignore that the acquisition of standards and patterns of behavior is also rooted in teaching.[26]

Let us ask ourselves, what images of the Church and home the normal Orthodox child will experience? Learning about his world and about himself is a long, slow process, but he does it by seeing, hearing, touching, tasting, and smelling in relationship to other people. Each bit of experience adds to others to help him find his place. For example, for a long time he feels himself to be part of his mother, but gradually he comes to realize that he is a separate self with eyes and ears which come to perceive his mother as a separate entity. He needs many, many experiences during his early years to discover himself and build self-esteem and self-confidence, without which we cannot speak of Christian nurture, but only of indoctrination. For educational purposes during early childhood, the handling of the world and its objects is primary and prior to naming them. This process normally becomes active just around eighteen months of age as the child develops his verbal skills. He must first feel at home with the objects before he can name them and certainly before he can conceptualize them. It is the personal and tactile contact with the Church that enables the child as person to develop a relationship with it and finally name it. This is essential for us as teachers and parents because it is the touch which precedes the conceptualization of the object. To encourage children to handle, to "taste and see," is to encourage them to learn meaningfully about them.

The religion of childhood is intuitive and concrete, not abstract and conceptual. It is not simply a smaller version of the adults' religion, but one which will simplify (read *distort*) whatever it cannot understand or deal with by centering on what is perceived as most obvious and focusing on it.

The child's job in the Orthodox setting is to make sense out of something by seeing how we adults deal with it and not by having it put into simpler words—hence, no children's churches or liturgies. This is not to suggest that the Orthodox child is to remain illiterate until he is thirteen— which would be true if cognitive development were the only criterion, as it is for most developmentalists. It does mean, however, that the child should be exposed to the fullness of the parish's social and liturgical experience as part of his "normal" Christian life. His being Orthodox is not defined by what he knows but by his shared membership in the body of Christ, the community of believers. Let the child learn through his senses, his natural way of learning; let him kiss his cross, taste the holy Eucharist, kiss the icons, light the candle, say the "magic" words of prayers before bed and meals—only let him say them together with mommy and daddy. Sophie Koulomzin writes: "In our Church all these physical objects, sensations and experiences are not merely religious baby-talk to be discarded later. Each of the things...remains a perfectly valid, meaningful action, gesture or experience through an Orthodox Christian's life."[26] He does not have to grow out of these to be a mature Christian—at twenty-two he will be doing the same things. He is, of course, in trouble if his understanding of these symbols and their meaning has not advanced beyond that appropriate for a three-year-old or a seven-year-old. What remains, whether or not we agree with developmental implications in religous education, is that the child's first experience of the Orthodox Church is his experience of its art, symbols, and stories.

In the case of young children the socialization process, of which art is but one aspect, begins *before* the person is capable of concrete or abstract reasoning, and in every case involves more than purely cognitive learning. The child identifies with the "significant others" in his life and with the manner in which they relate to the symbols and expect him to use the symbols. The symbols of the Church are carriers of meaning and tradition that speak to the whole person and not just the mind. The symbols call for a response, and their multivalent meanings allow for a variety of such responses from persons of different ages and personalities. The child sees how the symbols evoke actions and emotions from the parents. Gregory Baum sums up the function of religious symbols in the socialization process:

> Ever since we are [sic] little children, we are [sic] exposed to values, norms, meanings and purposes, through our parents and the social institutions...of which they are part, so that we assimilate a system of symbols long before we reach the rational maturity to be critical and search for our own values. Even when we reach this stage of maturity, we are never empty subjects in search of new meaning, for woven into our personal, intellectual, and emotional structure are the meaning and values in which we participated as we grew up....The symbol, then, expresses man's relationship to the ultimate in his life. The symbol makes this relationship more conscious and communicable, and thus intensifies man's involvement in it.[27]

What the child feels, tastes, smells, hears, and sees rapidly becomes a part of that child. The foundation of the scientific understanding of the child lies then in the child's sensory experience, which starts long before the school experience. Not through books or study but through the community of believers or the family is the faith of the Church communicated. The experiences of the first years of life are every bit as important as the school years, if not more so, for experiences are the stuff from which concepts are enabled to grow; they create the *disposition* to respond to God's love and grace.

Belonging

People, and this is particularly pronounced among adolescents, need to belong. The Church is the Church only as community, which by tradition lives in the past and by hope in the future. None of us stands alone before God; we are all part of the body, the Church. The experience of being part of a community belongs to the essence of spiritual growth. The infant or child deprived of the experience of belonging to a close, organized "family" unit is significantly handicapped. Doing something *together* at home or in the liturgy is extremely important, and all the traditions and celebrations go a long way toward establishing this sense of belonging. Children need a sense of belonging, accomplishment, and acceptance in the process of developing a sense of self-worth as a basis for faith (see John 10:11-15). This self-worth is not to be identified with a humanist, or Promethean, self-affirmation, but with a sense of his own acceptability before God. It is significant for us as educators, parents, and priests that the child with a healthy self-esteem is also the child who can risk trusting a God of love, can risk putting his faith into action.[28] Self-worth and self-esteem can only be nurtured in an active and caring community where the child is given responsibility in the life of that community and where he can trust the adults around him as reliable in their display of affection and consistent in their faith. Selma Fraiberg deals with the problem of non-attachment, which she refers to as a disease.[29] Non-attachment develops during the first eighteen months of life. What distinguishes the disease is the "incapacity of the person to form human bonds...." This will relate immediately to a later chapter on moral development; in the absence of normal human relationships it is difficult to form a conscience or develop the quality of self-observation, which is so foundational to spiritual life. We can only anticipate with great dread the results, both social and moral, of such early relationships.

Alienation arises when individuals perceive themselves as not sharing a common belief system, or a set of behavioral expectations and values, with others. Dr. Saul Levine, speaking at a symposium on "The Adolescent and Mood Disturbance," noted the damage done to adolescents by so-called "democratic-minded" parents who feel that it is wrong or antidemocratic to indoctrinate children by making behavioral demands on them and expressing a clear set of beliefs and values. The result is often a terrible, and frightening, sense of deracination. He suggests that belief and belonging are one step above the physical needs of people, but no less vital for functioning, competence, and adaptation.[30] The child must have a secure base from which to operate as he develops his own beliefs; freedom is an emotional illusion if there is no healthy core on which a child can build. This "healthy core" is the child's self-concept, shaped by his interaction with the home and the art, ritual, and music of the Church. He may well reject these roots—that is his prerogative, and we would not want Orthodox automatons who *carry* the faith of their parents but do not *possess* their own. Bear in mind that in adolescence, everything is up for grabs anyway as the youth gains a degree of autonomy. Expectations and traditions are the Church's way of saying what she intends for her faithful members by way of belief and behavior.

Identity Formation

Knowing how personality is formed is fundamental to any learning theory and to understanding how one grows into and identifies with the Church or any other community. To become a person, from a theological, sociological or anthropological perspective, is the gift of community. The paradigm of every community is the family, which, if healthy, becomes the archetype of all other social relationships, including the Church[31]—with the single significant exception that the Church, maintained as the body of Christ by the Holy Spirit, is an immediate horizontal and vertical relationship. But it starts in the home, ἐκκλησιούλα, which is a sacrament of common life, having its origin in marriage.

For Orthodox Christians, personhood is a central concept, a theological reality which took the Church several hundred years to define in an effort to describe who her Lord was. Membership in the Church and faith itself is a fundamentally relational and communal quantity—it is trust, the ability to trust in someone else, in the promise of someone else, in the constancy of someone else, which enables a person to live in faith in a world which oftentimes appears absurd. In a relationship with the people and symbols, on a sociological plane, of the ecclesiastical community, the foundation for a trusting life is laid. The personal relationship is particularly fundamental for the growth of the child as a healthy well-adjusted person as well as a person with the *potential* to respond in faith to God's loving kindness.

The relational nature of learning is absolutely fundamental to all human situations. It is not by accident that a close friend of mine, the principal of a so-called "problem school" in the Bronx, reports that his students learn much more effectively with computers than they do with "live" teachers. Of course they do! Since there is no basis for human interaction, there is no potential for conflict. For us Christians, it is self evident that genuine learning happens between and among people; each person in the learning relationship brings his own experiences of God and His Spirit, and this becomes part of the very content of what is in fact communicated. For Christians, the truth is never an abstraction, it is always personal because Christ, the truth, is a person. This is a fundamental learning condition with which we are "stuck." The favorite, "Jesus loves me, this I know, 'cause the Bible tells me so," is not terribly convincing to a child or an adult!

The question of socialization ultimately depends on the notion of personhood, not of knowledge. Personhood is basically a theological category, yet at the same time a social one, having its origin in relationships—that is, God in three persons relates to persons, saves them, loves them, heals them. James Fowler offers a brilliant note on the relational origin of self-identity or personhood: "Unless there are others who, by their constancy in caring for and interacting with us provide the feedback by which we can form reliable images of ourselves, we cannot develop and maintain identity."[32] This statement represents sound Orthodox personality theory, which has its roots in the primacy of the family, the first community, the ἐκκλησιούλα, which offers personhood to the infant as a gift of common life. Personality, by God's design, is a gift of community and is neither a given at birth nor an accident of time nor an innate (Freudian) development. Personhood enables us to seek after, to respond to, and maintain a life with God's life and with the lives of our brothers and sisters. A child develops the sense of his own personhood in the family and more specifically in relationship with the members of the family and the objects that characterize the values of that family—in this case the expressions of the family's faith. Here again, the symbolic arts of the Church play a major role.

Prayer in the Family

Certainly one of the most difficult questions to touch upon from the perspective of formal Christian education is that of teaching children to pray. It is perhaps second only to that of how to teach children "to have" faith. Prayer, like faith, always carries with it more than the noun would indicate grammatically; it carries with it the skill of determining which behaviors are indicative of attitudinal changes, those actions that hint at, point to, and are signs of genuine prayer and faith. That is, realistically speaking, there is no prayer, just as there is no faith, that is superficial. It must always be more than what you see on the surface or it must always intend to be more than what is on the surface, even if the subject of the prayer cannot conjure up "more" in his heart, mind, or soul. I am in no way an expert in prayer; but I am an expert in the difficulty of praying, and it is this expertise which is needed in this chapter.

It seems to me that we can pursue a two-fold approach to prayer. Prayer is rooted in the nurturing of life of the Christian family. This is prayer as *formational*. Prayer is communication; it is communication directed, however, towards the persons of the Trinity. We can as families and parishes predispose children and adults to prayer, admitting that we cannot guarantee the external or internal conformity to any "ideal." Both pastors and parents must be careful not to confuse, as we have apprently done in North America, liturgy with prayer so that attending a public worship service exempts us from personal "closet" prayer. Such an identification has become a serious deception, all the more serious inasmuch as the attitudes characteristic of genuine prayer are necessary for genuine liturgy. A predisposition towards prayer depends on the ability of the person to both sense awe and wonder and to communicate. Pedagogically speaking, the enabling mental and emotional faculties which permit one to pray to God our Father are the same as those which enable us to approach each other in the liturgy as well as the other as lover, husband, wife, or friend. That righteous man whose prayer "avails much" to the good will of the Father (James 5:16) is also the good neighbor. Therefore, the quality of the communal or parochial model is essential. It is the ability of the child to form relationships that conditions the nature of the child's prayer life, the ability to approach God spontaneously and not necessarily in formal and prescribed words. The beginning of prayer is the child's ability to look at the starry sky and say: "That's great. Thank God for all those stars." Educationally it is absolutely clear that what is taught is not a self-contained entity to itself; it is a reality that is conditioned by both the teacher and the student, the parent and the child.

Evangelization, or instruction, is the second foundation for considering prayer. Children learn formal prayers, and they learn them by rote memorization. Prayer of the formal variety is the Church's language; it is in prayer, and particularly the constant prayer of the Church, that the Church maintains her life with her Lord, Jesus Christ. Hence, the monastery is the powerhouse of the Church because it is at constant prayer, and in that sense it is a type of all social communities. It is not by accident that one of the reform principles of Orthodox social activism, as in St Basil the Great (fourth century) and St Athanasius of Constantinople (thirteeth-fourteenth centuries), was the monastic model. Let's not be deceived: the monasteries did not just pray in words, they were obliged to pray in work and righteousness so that they became what was called *ergasteria airetos*, workshops of virtue.

We introduce our children to formal prayer and the first one is, of course, the Lord's Prayer, the very prayer which Jesus taught us to pray when speaking to God our Father. He did not tell us to be spontaneous, but, precisely, to say "these" words. It is formal prayer, the prayer of the community, and especially the Lord's Prayer, which is the foundation of all personal and informal prayer. It is God himself who emboldens us to pray, to call him "Our Father," "Pappa," "Daddy." It is an emboldening which can speak to a receptive person, one who can believe that he is worthy, and we must refer back to a sense of self-esteem as the basis for self-confidence. This self-confidence does not make us deserve God's love, but it enables us to receive it as a gift. The child's sense of belonging is heightened by his ability to share our adult words with us, our liturgy, our prayer, and eventually make them his own. It is the sharing of ancient and fixed prayers that permits the child to come to a sense of belonging with the visible and invisible "friends" of God in his Church.

Through systematically interacting with the symbols, practices, and stories of the Church in the home and through perceiving how the family interacts with them, the child begins to develop a notion of "who he is" as an Orthodox. The child appropriates the symbols; in addition, the Church verbally assigns him an identity. A person in these terms becomes what he is named. A child consistently described as an Orthodox Christian learns to regard himself as an Orthodox and comes to know in a preconceptual way what is expected of him by way of belief, behavior, and action. He comes to know himself as John, Mary, George, who is an Orthodox Christian. This, of course, says nothing about the nature or quality of his faith-life. The degree to which his self-identity, *how he perceives himself*, converges with his spiritual identity, *his awareness of himself as an Orthodox*, determines his emotional as well as his spiritual health. The ultimate test of his perception of himself as a member of a group is the pattern of his life—work, study, recreation, etc. Faith can never hold an isolated place in our lives![33] It is, in fact, the unifying principle of all of life's disparate dimensions—a personal wholeness without

which a person is neither morally nor spiritually nor emotionally healthy.

Cultural patterns—especially art, ritual, and stories—and
institutions are formative agents of an individual's self-image
and world view. The phenomenon of Christian identity
emerges not from a classroom or school but from the dialectic between the person and the Church. In the process of
appropriating the symbols and eventually the meaning and
belief systems behind them, the child comes not only to
sense belonging, but also to *sense who he is*. The degree to
which he appropriates Orthodox symbols and relates to
them is the degree to which he perceives himself as
Orthodox and the degree to which he will believe and
behave as one. The beginning, spiritually and socially, is in
the home, with the appropriation of the Church's symbols,
values, and beliefs. Symbols enable the child or adult to
reach the reality within or behind the symbol as well as
achieve a sense of identity. The dynamic interaction between person and symbol is not just a preconceptual phase
that the child passes through—it is a constant element, the
Eucharist being the prime example, in the faith-life of the
person. Symbols are the presence of God. The child not
exposed to the presence of God will come to accept the
absence of God as real, and, gradually, what he accepts
psychologically may for him become ontologically true. The
child who experiences being part of the Church or the
family is given a solid foundation for Christian life long after
the schooling information has been forgotten. His faith is
then always the faith of the Church, which he has appropriated in a way unique to himself. Faith, however, is always a
mystery and a gift; discussion of it cannot be exhausted by
developmental or phenomenological descriptions, which
merely tell us *what* is happening, and not *why* or *how*.[34]
How is this faith appropriated? Again, St Basil gives us a

guideline: the local church must create "the disposition" ($\dot{\eta}$ $\delta\iota\acute{\alpha}\theta\epsilon\sigma\iota\varsigma$), the ambience in which faith can happen, or else any parish, of any quality, would be equally effective in nurturing faith.[35]

World Maintenance

The Orthodox Church believes that it has a message of eternal significance and, even more, that it is God's community, as was the Israel of the old covenant. Like every group that takes itself seriously, it has a mission, a responsibility, to transmit this living message to successive generations and to the "nations." Part of the function of the symbols is to help to maintain that message in a world of rapid change and overlapping and conflicting symbols. Their job is to hold together the Church's shared vision of reality, a vision born in the community's experience. This is not a question of conservatism but of faithfulness to an experience of reality perceived as correct. Church art, architecture, stories, and ritual practices are part of the Church's framework of meaning, which enables persons to make sense out of their lives and discern God's will in the midst of what often appears as an absurd life-experience. This symbolic constancy in a world of bewildering change can secure the person and the community.

Catechesis

This socialization model embraces historical, theological, and pedagogical elements of Christian nurture and Christian education. It takes the reality of the human experience of community, of the faith of the Church, and builds on that as a starting point for understanding belonging, self, faith, and world maintenance. It begins with the phenomena at hand—art, music, vestments, colors, tastes, and interpersonal relationships. While socialization may be the foundation, we can never forget that the Fathers always emphasized catechesis, the actual instruction in the appropriate subject at the appropriate time and place. The content of this instruction was always the foundations—knowledge of who God is, what he has done for us, and does for us in his Church. Without this understanding, the socialization model I am proposing would be little more than an aboriginal initiation rite. It is of note that the very success of the Christian Church in the fourth and fifth century Roman Empire put an end to the catechumenate and the end of catechesis as formal initiatory instruction. Nonetheless, the Church between the sixth and the fifteenth centuries managed to communicate its basic belief system and customs.[36] Ultimately there is a mutual interaction between nurture and catechesis: those who are efficiently catechized are those who will most probably nurture well; those who are nurtured well are usually those who will catechize well. We cannot afford to believe that nurture alone provides adequately for the educational ministry of the Church.[37]

The Orthodox child confronts a bewildering display of artifacts, actions, rites, movements, and discipline (e.g., fasting), and needs to make sense of these as he grows in maturity. He then observes what his parents do and what explicit demands they make on him—"kiss the icon," "kneel now," "make your cross." These all constitute the symbol system of the Orthodox Church and home, and they convey in a preconceptual way meanings, values, and beliefs. In other words, the Orthodox child finds a multifaceted and multivalent world of objects and rituals already externalized by previous generations as an expression of faith. He comes to know the Orthodox Church as an objectified world of structured meanings and patterns of behavior that he must now internalize as a member of a specific family which gives his life meaning and direction. The focus of any educational effort must not be on individuals, but on forming, informing and reforming the community of the family and the parish. Through these communities personalities are shaped and membership is created. We cannot reach our children or youth without ministering to their socializing elements. Finally, we must offer community skills ($\alpha i \tau \acute{\epsilon} \chi \nu \alpha \iota$) to families as part of a conscious effort to build (rebuild) healthy families as communities which have the Church as their focus.

Catechetically, we must bear in mind that the child is to be socialized into the *effects* of the Church—her actions, beliefs, calendar, art, music. He is not being given faith. Faith cannot be given by someone else, except the Spirit of God, and beliefs must not be confused with faith. Ultimately, being an Orthodox is more than using the right doctrines, the correct fingers, icons, rituals, music and architecture. Interlocking and mutually supportive beliefs, values, attitudes, behavior and artifacts cannot teach faith and must not be allowed to become in adulthood a substitute for faith. Faith is a gift of God and calls for a response that is unique to each person, and each person must be converted to his own relationship with Jesus Christ. The symbolic forms of the Church are, on the contrary, standardized. These ambient experiences of the symbols of the faith and their constancy in the home and Church provide one element in the dialectic of the development of a child's perception of belonging to that Church. And thus, the socialization paradigm of Christian education permits us to focus on the tangible relations of the person with the Church as a basis ($\delta \iota \acute{\alpha} \theta \epsilon \sigma \iota s$) for faith.

Chapter 2 Footnotes

[1]Robert O'Neil and Michael Donovan, *God, Church, and Children* (New York: World, 1970), 91.

[2]On the categories of autonomy and heteronomy in moral and emotional development, see Ronald Duska and Mariellen Whelan, *Moral Development: A Guide to Piaget and Kohlberg* (New York: Paulist Press, 1975), 9-20. On the influence of John Dewey's progressive model of the child as a "developing person," see John H. Westerhoff III, *Will Our Children Have Faith* (New York: Seabury Press, 1980), 8-9.

[3]See St Basil of Caesarea, *The Long Rules*, in *The Fathers of the Church*, series 9, tr. Monica Wagner (New York: Fathers of the Church, Inc., 1950), 248-252. I am indebted to the Rev. Dr. Joseph Allen, who brought this and the following reference to my attention in an unpublished paper entitled "The Pastoral Dimension in the Writings of St. Basil the Great."

[4]*Homily 13 on Psalm 28*, in *Fathers of the Church*, series 46, tr. Agnes Way (Washington, D.C.: Catholic University of America Press, 1963), 195.

[5]Berard Marthaler, "Socialization as a Model for Catechetics," in *Foundations of Religious Education*, ed. Patraic O'Hare (New York: Paulist Press, 1978), 64-92. On the use of the term "socialization," see J.A. Clausen, "A Historical and Comparative View of Socialization Theory and Research," in *Socialization and Society*, ed. J.A. Clausen (Boston: Little, Brown and Co., 1964); and T.K. Danzinger, *Socialization* (Baltimore: Penguin, 1971). The term is much misused, as, I believe, when O'Neil and Donovan write that "Catechesis is the most important form of socialization and initiation into the subculture of Catholicism" (13). Catechesis is defined as the "formal passing on of the communities' faith story" and, in fact, plays a minor role in socialization into any religious subculture in North America.

[6]Westerhoff, 80-6.

[7]In this author's opinion, this is one of the weaknesses of Westerhoff's treatment. The "community" he discusses, into which the child is being integrated, is not defined other than as a horizontal reality, as an association of people who believe they are God's people. Clearly, his community-of-faith is not the Church, and the tradition(s) to which he refers are never defined. See Westerhoff, 72.

[8]Ibid., 102. Westerhoff spaces the "initiation" sacraments—baptism, communion and confirmation—throughout the child's early years. First communion, for example, is scheduled sometime around the second grade (age 7), because it is at that time that a child is capable of so-called "affiliative" faith, i.e., consciousness of sharing something with a group (94). Similarly, confirmation is administered in "early adulthood," when a child is capable of "owned faith" (98). This selection is arbitrary and again indicative of his inability to deal with the vertical dimension of church life—i.e., it is God's grace that makes "membership" in his Church possible.

[9]Ibid., 56-7.

[10]It is worth noting in this regard that the curriculum of the Orthodox Christian Commission for grades N through 9, which this author had some hand in determining, is heavily liturgical, with an almost embarrassing absence of any ethical, moral or spiritual emphasis.

[11]P.L. Berger and T. Luckman, *The Social Construction of Reality* (New York: Anchor Books, 1967), 61-2.

[12]Marthaler, 70.

[13]See Kathrene M. Tobey, *Learning and Teaching through the Senses* (Philadelphia: Westminster Press, 1970), 17: "Sensory learning is basic for persons of all ages." Westerhoff refers to the absence of this as "skin hunger," the need for which is satisfied among American teens and adults by antisocial punching and jabbing.

[14]Norma Thompson, "Current Issues in Religious Education," *Religious Education 72* (November-December 1978), 626.

[15]John Dillenberger, "Religion and the Sensibilities of the Artist," *Liturgy and Form 12* (Autumn 1978), 13.

[16]Paul F. Grendler, "The Schools in Christian Doctrine in Sixteenth Century Italy," *Church History* 53, (1984), 307-318.

[17]See Philip Greven, *The Protestant Temperament* (New York: Alfred Knopf, 1980), 172-173.

[18]Marie Winn, *Children Without Childhood* (New York: Pantheon Books, 1983), 75-83.

[19]On the centrality of play to normal moral and human development as well as its contribution towards socialization and the development of conscience, Marie Winn's *Children Without Childhood* is a must reading for concerned educators and parents.

[20]Frank Nelson "Aesthetic Dimension in Christian Education," *Religious Education 66* (September-October 1971), 385-9.

[21]Lukas Vischer, "Introduction into the Life of Faith in the Early Church," *RISK 2* (1966), 46-57.

[22]G. Bareille, "Catechumenat," in *Dictionnaire de théologie catholique* (Paris, 1910) 2:1968, 1971-7. The nurturing nature of the educational process is especially evident in Cyril of Jerusalem for whom the reality of the sacramental experience is the basis for catechesis. That is, the *photizomenoi* are first to experience the sacraments and then have them explained, as he does in that portion of his *Catechetical Oration* known as the *Mystagogical Catechesis*.

[23]Ronald Goldman, *Religious Thinking from Childhood to Adolescence* (New York: Seabury Press, 1965), 220-4. See also John Elias, *Psychology and Religious Education* (Bethlehem, Pa.: Catechetical Communications, 1975), 54-6; and Sam Keen's critique of James Fowler's faith development stages in Fowler and Keen, *Life Maps: Conversations on the Journey of Faith* (Minneapolis: Winston Press, 1978), 102-29.

[24]Grendler, *op.cit.*

[25]David Elkind, "The Role of Play in Religious Education," *Religious Education 75* (May-June 1980), 282.

[26]See Selma Fraiberg, *The Magic Years* (New York: Scribner's Sons, 1959), 148; *idem, Every Child's Birthright* (New York: Basic Books, 1977), 27.

[26]Koulomzin, 36-7. On the centrality of digital manipulation in human mental and intellectual development, see Maria Montesorri, *The Absorbent Mind* (New York: Delta Books, 1967), 148-57.

[27]Gregory Baum, "Truth in the Church—Kung, Rahner, and Beyond," *The Ecumenist* (March-April 1971), 43; see also the same author's *Religion and Alienation* (New York: Paulist Press, 1975), 238-65.

[28]Jan Chartier, "Every Child: Someone Special," *Baptist Leader* (July 1980), 50-3.

[29]Fraiberg, *Birthright*, 45-62; *idem, Magic Years*, 148.

[30]Reported in Saul Kappel, "Sense of Belonging Vital to Adolescents," New York *Daily News* (May 27, 1980), 38. Also on belonging, see Merton Strommen, *Five Cries of Youth* (New York: Harper and Row, 1979), 1-32.

[31]See St John Chrysostom, *Homilies on Timothy* 10, in *Nicene and Post-Nicene Fathers* (Grand Rapids: Eerdmans, 1969), Series 1, Vol. 13, 437-441.

[32]Fowler and Keen, 19. See ibid., 17-20, on faith as a verb and faith as a "relational" category.

[33]C. Ellis Nelson, *Where Faith Begins* (Richmond, Va.: John Knox Press, 1967), 188-203.

[34]It is of note that Fowler's entire discussion of faith development makes no mention of either God's action or faith as a gift. Faith is an action state which may or may not be directed toward God.

[35]See St Basil of Caesarea, *The Moral Rules* 80:22, in *Fathers of the Church*, series 9, 203-4.

[36]Milton McC. Gatch, "The Ancient Church," in John H. Westerhoff (ed.), *A Faithful Church* (Wilton, CT: Morehouse-Barlow Co., 1981), 80.

[37]For a warning concerning the over emphasis on the socialization model at the expense of what he refers to as "evangelization," see John. H. Westerhoff, *op.cit.*, 5.

CHAPTER 3

The Family as Educator

Family life for the Christian tradition is based on the fundamental first principle of the social nature of fully human existence. Here I will consider the Christian family as the matrix for the nurturing of Christian personality characteristics. I will consider these characteristics as being pre-theological, inasmuch as they are foundational for later spiritual and religious development.

We Orthodox face a number of problems that are not inherent in the nature of the family itself, but in the Church's failure to reflect critically on the family as the matrix of trust, personhood, and intimacy, rather than merely the locus of information and values. There was seemingly no problem with this assumption as long as there was a *corpus Christianum* and an economic necessity that forced people to live together in permanent units.

In the formative period of the Church's life there was no formal thinking on the nature of family, marriage, or community. With the exception perhaps of the lives of saints, secondhand information in historical sources, and the writings of a few Fathers (such as Gregory of Nyssa's eulogy on his father's death), no treatment exists of the goals of family living. The family was treated as a constant, self-evident reality whose fundamental theological justification was that of Ephesians 5:31-32:

> For this cause shall a man leave his father and his mother, and shall be joined unto his wife, and they two shall be one flesh. This is a great mystery: but I speak concerning Christ and the Church.

The tradition concerning marriage and the family has been both positive and negative. On the one hand, it revealed an infatuation with virginity as the preferred state, as in Matthew 19:12, I Corinthians 7:38, and Revelation 4:4. The superiority of virginity was praised in the *Shepherd of Hermas* (Similitude ix, chs 8, 24)[1], and Justin Martyr spoke of the elderly who remained pure and uncorrupted (*Apology* 1:15).[2] Certainly, this tradition proved unfavorable to family life! This negative tendency was so evident that the Church had occasionally to affirm the acceptability of marriage and family life. Canons 4 and 9 of Gangra (ca 325-381), for instance, condemned anyone who rejected marriage or pursued virginity because he deemed marriage unclean.[3] Canon 15 of the same Council of Gangra condemned anyone who refused to nurture his children and "shall neglect them, under pretense of asceticism.[4]

On the other hand, the Church has tended also to idealize the family as the perfect form of community in which Christians can experience the fullest possible expression of Christian mutuality. Although the tendency to affirm the family was most evident in the Old Testament,[5] St Paul accentuated this trend with his identification of the husband/wife relationship with that of the Christ/Church relationship. This particular reference, in Ephesians 5, was in fact the basis for the later Byzantine treatment of marriage as a sacrament(al). St John Chrysostom continued this, emphasizing the family as the *ekklesioula*, the *little church*: "For indeed the household is a little Church."[6] Again, John Chrysostom in his Commentary on Ephesians urged husbands to "imitate the bridegroom of the Church."[7] Although there is little critical material on the nature of the family or its educational function in the Fathers and almost nothing in the canons, Meyendorff has noted that this was not because they were indifferent to its form or content:

> Never, in her entire history, did the Christian Church show more clearly that she was bringing into the world a new and unprecedented divine reality and presence.[8]

While this approach may have been positive, it has also tended to be stress-producing. There is no such reality as the family *in abstracto*. The application of this idealized perspective to the family in its nuclear form has increased the strain on an already over-burdened institution. It is in the context of the failure of the nuclear family to live up to the ideals established for it and keep its promises as a mutualistic community that we witness among adolescents the fascination with cults and sects, and the epidemic increase in suicide. People are looking elsewhere for the validation and sense of belonging that the nuclear family is hard pressed to provide.

The Church's failure to produce a community of trained theologians, educators, and sociologists to consider the family has prevented the Orthodox community in North America from working for an effective family-centered and family-life catechesis. We Orthodox possess no guidelines on the family or family education. When formal thinking does occur, it is invariably in terms of pious affirmation of the family that serves to increase the stain as we compare the *is* and the *ought* of the actual experience. With the exception of contemporary works by Meyendorff and Constantelos,[9] which treat marriage historically, family life, Christian nurture, and parenting have been given short shrift in ecclesiastical tradition and current theological writing. Within the next generation the Church in North America must crystallize its theology of the family and parenting in light of the social sciences; without this educators and parents cannot speak of a meaningful family-life or family-centered ministry. This chapter will provide some practical and speculative reflections on the family as nurturer. The approaches here may be inchoate and eclectic, but such is the process of building Orthodox religious education. To be effective as a discipline and as a service to the Orthodox community, religious education must continually formulate theories and articulate traditional beliefs in the context of contemporary needs, issues, and research. To this theologians must respond in an effort to develop a biological model of the Orthodox family as educator.

The child's primary world, both psychologically and spiritually, is the family. Orthodox in North America have traditionally affirmed the importance of the family, but have done little about it. We tend to put our money on what we believe, and we have invested very little in family life education or family-centered catechesis.

> We need to recall that the family is the nuclear center from which all values arise and that even the child's later attendance at school does not annul the family's dynamic impact on his life.[10]

In this process of restoring the parents to their primary place as educators, we must first come to an understanding of the family, its functions, its theological and sociological imperatives, and the systems of which it is part and by which it is constituted. We can call upon the assistance of the social sciences to articulate a contemporary theological rationale for an institution that has been the single most constant feature of both human and Christian life. I have suggested above that the primary focus of our attention, and one in keeping with Orthodox history, tradition, and liturgical categories, is a socialization model as outlined by such educators as C. Ellis Nelson, John T. Westerhoff III, and Berard Marthaler.[11] In addition, developmental psychologists such as Piaget, Erikson, and Kohlberg are valuable to Christian educators and pastors for their findings on the internal dynamics—cognitive, emotional, and moral—of the individual and the manner in which these enable the family and its members to grow, develop, and respond to the word of God.

First let us develop a definition of "family," since for many Christian educators and sociologists the very definition runs the gamut from the specific to the absurdly general. For the purposes here, I will define family as any group of people, related by blood or will, living together in an intentionally permanent relationship, with or without children, whose bond has been sealed by a commitment to maintaining a community which is at once intimate and nurturing. The Orthodox will necessarily add that such a community must exist within the context of the Church—that is, the couple acting as the focal point must be heterosexual and must have sought out the blessing of Christ for the establishment of their community. These definitions are highly problematical inasmuch as the expectations of an Orthodox family are formally more specific and rigid than those for a non-Orthodox family. But for both the key elements are permanency, intimacy, heterosexuality, and recognition through a common liturgical (public) blessing.[12] Regardless of current definitions or redefinitions, the basic elements have not changed.

The definition offered here is the only one in my experience that allows for a meaningful theological and sociological discussion. The family may take a variety of forms fitting this general definition. It may be a single-parent family with multiple siblings; it may be a dual-parent family; it may be a childless couple; there may be relatives attached to it, either by blood or desire; it may be churched or unchurched; it may be hurting with emotional or physical handicaps. This definition does not presume to include only those groups that are functioning well either socially or spiritually, but does assume that the family in its essence must intend to be a community. Without this communal emphasis we cannot speak of the basic goal of Christian marriage or family, providing trust, intimacy, and growth of personhood as foundational for theosis.[13]

Regardless of its specific form, quality, or spiritual or emotional ambiguity, the family is the foundation of human life. It is the basic biological unit which has served humanity since the beginning of civilization in socializing its children and making traditions of its cultural or spiritual life. In spiritual and Scriptural tradition, the family is the paradigm of all communities and all love. Love for humankind grows not as an abstraction, but in the immediacy and intensity of family life; it is this love that is the foundation of our love for God (I John 4:21). Any institution, including the Church, is a community inasmuch as it manifests the qualities of the "family." The "family" of God means little except in the context of that human community created between two people within a system of larger relationships that define its internal dynamics and open it to the world outside of it.

The Christian family must have its focus outside of itself in another, transcendent reality; it is this "other" reference point that enables it to focus on spiritual or social realities. There can be no genuine community composed of possessive individuals.[14]

> Christianity breaks open the family, especially the
> extended family, and sees it as secondary to the

Kingdom. The family is a means and not an end.[15]

The family is community par excellence; but it is also community disabled by sin. It remains a human community with all its limitations and potential. Even though the family as educator is usually treated in the ideal, it cannot be discussed apart from the "fallen" nature of the world. After almost two acts of intra-familial plots, fratricides, adulteries, sibling rivalries, and intense family hatreds, James Goldman's *The Lion In Winter* portrays Eleanor of Aquitaine as saying "Well, what family doesn't have its ups and downs."[16]

This ambiguity does not contradict the centrality of the family in Christian life as a formative agency. The family is potentially the place where men and women learn to be men and women.[17] People are by their nature communal. Even celibacy or monasticism makes sense only in the context of the family as a mutualistic paradigm and is justified only in the context of the fallen world, a world misshapen by sin and separation. In a world whose purpose was clear and uni-directional, the family would be the norm as the Genesis account makes clear (Genesis 2:18). The fact remains that historically the Church institutionalized celibacy in a communal format, in the *cenobium* — the anchorite remaining the rare, albeit venerated, exception to the rule of communal existence. St Basil the Great, the father of eastern and to an extent western monasticism, describes his monastic community in the mutualistic terms of family life. The goal of any community is nurture for salvation. For St Basil the *cenobia* are, like families, communities in which men and women can and must struggle with being human, social, and sinful. What is there about community/family that is both fundamental and foundational for spiritual and pre-theological development? St Basil here offers significant insight into the social analogies of spiritual growth:

I consider that life passed in company with a

number of persons in the same habitation (striving
for the same objective) is more advantageous than
the life of the solitary in many respects. My reasons
are (1) that no one of us is self-sufficient as regards
corporeal necessities, but we require one another's aid in supplying our needs....Similarly, (2) in
the solitary life, what is at hand becomes useless to
us and what is wanting cannot be provided, since
God, the Creator, decreed that we should require
the help of one another, as it is written, so we
might associate with one another [Ecclesiastes
13:20]....And again, (3) the doctrine of charity of
Christ does not permit the individual to be concerned solely with his own private interests....
Furthermore, (4) a person living in solitary retire-
ment will not readily discern his own defects,
since he has no one to admonish and correct him
with mildness and compassion....Moreover, (5)
the majority of the commandments are easily
observed by several persons living together, but
not so in the case of one living alone....Besides, (6)
if all we who are united in the hope of our calling
[Ephesians 4:4] are one body with Christ as our
Head, we are also members one of another [I
Corinthians 12:12]....In addition, (7) since no one
has the capacity to receive all spiritual gifts, but the
grace of the Spirit is given proportionally to the
faith of each [Romans 12:6], when one is living in
association with others, the grace privately bes-
towed on each individual becomes the common
possession of his fellows....each employs his own
gift to enhance it by giving others a share, besides
reaping benefits from the gifts of others as if they
were his own.[19]

We find here in St Basil a brilliant rationale, both sociological and spiritual, for the common life. He is the spokesman of
social mutuality, and each of his seven points, whether on
the social, emotional, or spiritual plane, can be applied
equally to the married or to the monastic. The family then is

not a hurdle to be overcome on the way to salvation, not a barrier to the Kingdom, but the very matrix of that salvation and locus of that Kingdom. It is clear for Basil: the social is not accidental to humankind; it is not *bene esse*, but *esse*.

The same emphasis on mutualism is evident in St Clement of Alexandria, who writes: "We admire monogamy and the high standing of single marriage, holding that we ought to share suffering with another and bear one another's burdens, [Galatians 6:2], lest anyone who thinks he stands secure of himself should fall."[19] Clement goes on to affirm that "both celibacy and marriage have their own different forms of service and ministry to the Lord."[20]

The family must be discussed, first, in the context of faith, growth, and Christian nurture and, second, in terms of learning or education. If the family is the educator of first resort, the educator par excellence, it is so not in terms of any schooling-instructional paradigm, but in terms of a socialization paradigm that refers to the family as the place where the ability to have faith is born and nurtured in a community of intimacy. John H. Westerhoff in his *Will Our Children Have Faith?*[21] affirms what we all—parents, priests, and teachers—have intuited, but never acted on: You cannot teach children faith, but you can teach them *about* religion.[22] Faith comes as a gift of God to a person willing/able to receive it; such is the Orthodox doctrine of synergistic anthropology.[23] There are sound theological, spiritual, and pedagogical reasons for this distinction. First, faith cannot be taught; it comes as an unmerited gift of God to an "open" person, who must be able and willing to cooperate with it. The foundations for this *synergeia*—trust, personhood, intimacy—are laid in the family. There will be objections that grace cannot be limited! True. The fact remains, however, that our ability to receive grace and our willingness to cooperate with it are factors that cannot be ignored without contradicting the reality of human freedom and the structure of human development in communities.

Second, the material of Christian learning, like that of secular learning—dates, numbers, names—cannot and should not be taught by parents. Schooling in the informational, instructional sense does not properly belong to parents! This conclusion may be violated only at the risk of great harm to sound educational principles as well as to the parents' mental health. The experience of this writer and many educators is that parents do not have sufficient objectivity to assume a didactic role with their own children. The role of the family in the nurturing (formation) of its members, both young and old, is far more foundational than any didactic function it might try to serve. It is this last point that I will seek to develop in the remainder of this chapter.

The first objective of the ministry of the family is the growth and nurture of healthy personalities. A healthy personality is the product of a healthy family; a healthy Christian personality is the product of a healthy Christian family. The family is the best learning situation precisely because in it human interaction is both intensive and extensive; the family is the primary determinant of the child's later religious and spiritual life, attitudes, and beliefs. The type of teaching that makes for Christian growth—spiritual and moral—can only occur in the family as in the community described above by St Basil. In fact, Christian education did not move into the schooling-instructional paradigm until the sixteenth century when education in a didactic sense became one of the tools of propaganda for the churches of both the Reformation and the Counter Reformation. It did not characterize the Eastern Church, by design or accident; it certainly did not characterize the early Church. On the early Church, Henry Marrou has written:

> Christian education of children, through which

they learn to share in the treasury of the faith, to submit to a healthy discipline in the matters of morals, was the parents' fundamental duty. There was more in this than was contained in the Roman tradition: it was essentially a continuation of the Jewish tradition, which emphasized the importance of the family in the development of religious consciousness. And this duty could not be delegated; the early Church would have had sharp words to say about "Christian" parents of today who think they have done all that is required of them when they have passed their children over to a teacher or an institution.[24]

Baptism and the Family

We begin with baptism, the beginning of life for the Christian person. By the baptismal event we are reborn or born anew into God's family. It is only in the perspective of the theology of baptism, chrismation, and eucharist, the "sacrament" of initiation, that we can build a theory and practice for family-life and family-centered catechesis. The act, however, is essentially meaningless unless the child's parents and godparents bear the faith of the Church and are themselves faithful. We must as pastors, parents, and educators ask what the act of baptism means when the parents are not faithful Orthodox. It is only because of the faith of the family that a child can be offered for baptism at all?[25] Infant baptism can be justified only in the context of the solidarity of the family. With all due respect to the power of God's love and grace, the baptism of the child is immediately related to the faith of the parents; he is baptized by the faith of his parents, possessing none properly of his own. After the act of baptism the child is largely a passive participant in a process whereby the parents agree that they will be responsible for his nurture in the faith of the Church. The faith, however, is modeled by the behavior of the parents; in a real sense the faith is enfleshed in their lives and, for the child, only in them.[26] Peer-group influence is very often by default and may in fact by considerable only by passive neglect.[27]

Many sociological studies, especially those of Andrew Greeley and William McCready affirm that the influence of the family far exceeds the traditional claims that the family is a model in the formative years and that its influence is far greater than any influence that peers might have.[28] Greeley and Rossi have found, for instance, that the "religiousness" of adults was greater when they were raised in a family where there was a "lively" faith.

> If our data from the past are any indication of the present situation, Catholic education is virtually wasted on three-fourths of those in Catholic schools because of the absence of a sufficiently religious family milieu.[29]

The family is not just the principle educator but the educator of such importance that the influence of all other factors is at best marginal. Potvin, Hoge, and Nelson, in a study for Boys Town Center for the Study of Youth Development and the Catholic University of America, conclude:

> The most important predictors of religiosity as measured by these indices (religious behavior) are parental religious practice and whether or not the adolescent is currently studying religion.... Nonetheless these appear to be no substitute for a religious home environment and for religious instruction if adolescents are to remain committed to their religious heritage.[30]

Note that no one is here speaking of the development of faith. The family, as the Church, cannot impose faith or force it; it can only set the stage to allow grace to work in the life of the child.[31] For the Fathers of the Church grace was not a thing, but an encounter, a meeting with the living person, Jesus Christ. The aim of Christian life and nurture is to permit the growth of theosis through a life-long encounter with Christ. Correct doctrine is valuable not as an academic excercise, but as a model which arises from faith and at the same time allows faith to happen. From the human side of *synergeia*, I would suggest that this encounter exercises the same emotional and personality faculties as are employed in a normal personal relationship.

Dethroning the Children

The contemporary sociological findings on the influence of the family are both sobering and exciting; their weakness, however, is that they continue to treat family and marriage in terms of children. In the tradition of the Church, the consensus seems to be that children are necessary to family life, but not sufficient. Marriage and physical love are not justified by children! Elchaninov writes:

> In fleshly love, besides its intrinsic value as such, God has granted the world a share in His own omnipotence: man creates man, a new soul is brought into being.[32]

The wedding ceremony implies that the relationship will come to fruition in child bearing and rearing; there is, however, no sufficiency in this. At least by implication the meaning of marriage changes from the Old Testament to the New Testament, which nowhere focuses on procreation as the justification for marriage. "Not a single New Testament text mentioning marriage points to procreation as its justification or goal."[33] Meyendorff further asserts this interpretation by noting that Christ's prohibition of divorce, except in cases of fornication (Matthew 5:32; 19:9; Mark 10:11; and Luke 16:18), indicates that the relationship between husband and wife is eternal and an end in itself; it cannot be clouded by necessities such as posterity or family solidarity (as in Judaism). Again, Elchaninov comments:

Marriage, fleshly love, is a very great sacrament and mystery. Through it is accomplished the most real and at the same time the most mysterious of all possible forms of human relationships. And, qualitatively, marriage enables us to pass beyond all the normal rules of human relationship and to enter a region of the miraculous, the superhuman.[34]

The family, then, has children but is not defined by children. The schooling-instructional paradigm has emphasized the family in terms of its service to its children; this, in my opinion, is a distortion of the New Testament and patristic understanding of the family. The fact is that the family does not exist for its children; it exists for all its members, but especially for the spouses, and their mutual love. If their mutual love is an exclusive, closed-in relationship, however, it is demonic. Certainly, one of the legitimate functions of the family is the nurturing of its children, but it is not its only function; if it were, we would have to conclude that marriage, including the sexual contact that legitimately expresses that love, should come to an end along with the desire and ability to bear children. Similarly, it is not by accident that the duration of many modern marriages seems to be that of childhood, the end of which signals the end of the parents' life together. It is my conclusion that what keeps parishes from giving attention to family-centered and family-life catechesis is the difficulty in most people's minds of separating religious education from its associations with childhood. Presumably, people without children should not be part of a family-life or family-centered program.

On the basis of traditional belief and modern research, it is time to move away from the sixteenth-century emphasis on childhood education, away from a child-centered and content-centered to a family-centered and family-life catechesis. The Orthodox Church behaves as if becoming a member of the Church was always a schooling enterprise. A sense of desperation forces us to see the child as the end of the educational process rather than the beginning. The sooner we break the mold, given the tendency to teach as we were taught, the more effective will be the Church's educational ministry.

Family Systems: A Proposal for Parish Planning

The family is made up of members who relate to one another and to those outside of the family through a complicated series of interactions. People do not live in one particular social situation or in one dimension of a social situation; they rather tend to play an increasing number of roles in an increasingly complex societal structure. On the positive possibilities of these interactions, Meyendorff alludes to a similar effect:

> [The Fathers of the Church] knew, sometimes much better than modern psychologists, that the human instinct of love and procreation is not isolated from the rest of human existence, but is its very center.[35]

Thus, it is particularly valuable to consider systems thinking and the relatively recent study of family as parts of systems. The systems approach, distantly derived from operations research during the Second World War and more proximately from the computer industry, eschews Cartesian isolation of phenomena in favor of a holistic and contextual approach to components. For the parish planning a family-centered and family-life ministry a systems approach permits focus on the experience of the family as center to each of its members and focus on the family as part of the Church and society. The complexity of the interpersonal interactions within the family and between the family and the world around it enables us to look on it as a system much like other systems. "It is axiomatic in systems thinking about family that the disturbance/dysfunction of one member manifests a group problem."[36] Samuel Natale of Fordham University's Graduate School of Religon and Religious Education writes.

> Recently psychological thinking, especially in the field of systems theory, confirms what common sense has told us all along: the family is the institution primarily responsible for the development of its members, particularly in their formative years.[37]

Natale, a specialist in human development, emphasizes the multi-relational nature of the familial community. Family systems enable educators and pastors to see people in the context of the web of relationships in which they live, learn, and grow. As will be emphasized later, the quality and nature of these various relationships determine the foundational pre-theological traits for the development of faith-life.

A systems approach enables us to see children in a larger perspective as part of a complicated series of relationships that condition their development rather than as an isolated group to be "schooled" out of childhood and into Christianity. In addition to helping us focus on the child as a dynamic interactant in the family, a systems approach enables us to view the educational enterprise as encompassing the entire family, several or more families, the neighborhood, the parish, the public school, social service agencies, and so forth. In fact, my experience in Christian education has been that Orthodox ignore this systems approach in spite of the tight ethnic nature of their communities. This creates the web of relationships that support an effective educational ministry to the whole person. Our tendency to focus on the child, instead of the family, has forced us into the pattern of education that ignores systems and violates what we believe about the family, the child, and the nature of the local eucharistic community. We have, in fact, focused so intensely on the child and childhood education that the parish itself has contributed to the family's disorientation. Through its child-centered education program and its emphasis on the schooling-instructional paradigm at the expense of worship, the parish has, for example, separated the members of the family at precisely the time when they are the family par excellence, in the eucharistic celebration. The school model would in itself be tolerable, if in implementing the model the children were not isolated from the rest of the parish and the common worship of the Church; when they do attend, they invariably do so as a distinct group, not sitting with their parents. Instead we have come to dissociate family ministry from childhood education, as if the latter were an untouchable divine given. If it is untouchable, it is because we have no perspective—either sociological, theological, or historical—for another approach.[38]

When we discuss the family as a teaching/learning agency, we are obliged to consider its potential for all its members. A family systems approach enables us to start from a sound theological and sociological perspective and to treat the various relationships that together constitute family life. These relationships include those between spouses as parents, between spouses as lovers, between parents and children, between mother and children, between father and children, as well as those innumerable possible relationships outside of the immediate family unit with other families, children, the parish priest, and institutions, community agencies, the parish, and neighbors. Finally, it includes the relationship of the family members to the faith of the Church, the *paradosis*, as well as the community of the faith. A systems approach enables us to understand the socialization model as the one most adequate to the nurturing process in the Orthodox faith.[39] An educational ministry focusing on the family as a system and as part of systems is the foundational perspective for family-centered and family-life catechesis.

The nature of an educational program depends on the relationship on which the parish chooses to focus as central at a particular time and place. If, as I am doing here, we are talking about the ministry of the family to its members (family-centered catechesis), then a program for spouses as parents might focus on parenting skills and moral development; a program for teens might focus on morality and getting along with parents. What a family systems approach helps us to do is to break the family down into its various aspects and to treat them in relationship to one another. It reminds us that the family is not a monolith, with an immediate relationship to God and isolated from the rest of the social or parochial order; neither is it the romanticized ideal imagined by celibates and lovers. The family as community is a combination of needs and interests which can become the occasion for an effective family-life or family-centered ministry if we only recognize the interconnectedness of the unit. Once we treat it as a system, we can break out of the mystique of the family as an isolated and perfect nuclear unit. Only when we see it as real (related) and fallen can we facilitate its functioning.

Relationships Within the Family

Religious socialization is a process concerned with the origins of religious thought, attitudes, and behaviors, and how and to what extent these are transmitted through the family from one generation to another. To the extent that this does not happen, we have a rootless family, a family whose members are out of touch with their spiritual heritage and consequently have no direction. John Elias of Fordham has written:

> Socialization takes place within the family because children so identify with the family as a group that its ways become part of their own selves. The family is the first reference group whose values, norms, and practices one assimilates and uses to evaluate the values, and behavior of others.[40]

The pattern of interaction that children see within the family become models for their own interaction with others. We have long known that the young child is a product of the interaction with his parents and other siblings. Researchers have come to realize that the quality of the development was dependent on the quality of the relationship between the two parents as determinants for the ambience of the family unit.[41] Hence, from a spiritual, emotional, and pedagogical point of view the single most significant relationship in the child's life is that between his mother and his father, contrary to the common belief that it is the one between the child and the mother; the parents' mutual love, sharing, concern, affection, ability to talk and to serve one another's needs are most significant in the child's formation as a person. Lucie Barber writes of the research of Tiltz:

> [At Notre Dame] he began researching the development of the young child. Basically, the research suggested that the young child was a product of the interaction of himself and his parents along with the siblings. Happy with this insight, Tiltz then began to realize that the quality of the interaction was dependent upon the quality of the interaction between the husband and wife. This was precedent to the interaction with the child and also was the dependent factor as to the quality of the parental interaction with the young child in the developing of his/her self-concept.[42]

These findings have been refined and applied to Roman

Catholic families by William McCready, who discovered that the quality of intimacy of the parental relationship has a significant impact on the religious socialization of the child.

> Those families in which the parents have a warm and loving relationship provide a more secure base for the loving transmission of basic value orientation, especially those concerning the importance and meaning of life which are symbolized in religious attitudes and behaviors.[43]

He continues that the "quality of parental relationship is often a stronger predictor of adolescent behavior than is parental behavior itself."[44] This is a sobering conclusion for parents who have long believed that children pay more attention to what parents do vis-a-vis the Church than to how they behave toward one another.

Even more significant for parents and priests, but certainly in keeping with the earlier tradition of the Church and the ecclesiastical role of men in general, is the significance of the father in the development of the children's life of faith. Recent studies indicate the centrality of the father in the religious development and nurturing of both male and female children.[45] Andrew Greeley has taken up McCready's research and notes that:

> An analysis of the parochial school data by my colleague, William McCready, leaves no doubt at all that the most important predictor of religious performance of children is the religious behavior of their parents (and particularly their fathers) and the quality of the relationship between their mothers and fathers.[46]

If McCready's and Greeley's research is valid, they will have demonstrated that parents, and particularly the fathers, are so fundamental to spiritual and religious development that all other institutions can effectively be considered marginal.

The father's role has from the time of the early Church

eroded to the point where education and even attendance and membership is seen primarily as a female function. To a great extent the immigrant mentality among the Orthodox has accelerated the erosion of male leadership/presence in the family. Perhaps the first step to a renewal of family life, generally, and family-life catechesis, specifically, is the creation of an awareness among fathers of their spiritual importance. More must be expected of fathers than fellowship meetings and building maintenance committees. Certainly, the first step is to educate them[47] about their own importance and, second, to design programs on the parish level to enable fathers to fulfill their roles as spiritual leaders more responsibly. We will find that fathers, like most people, are eager to learn to do a job better if they know what that job is and that they can be successful at it. Education for role-fulfillment is self-motivating.

These findings fit well with this writer's experience that Christianity is an adult's religion; its concepts and stories are not suited to the child's mental structure. The child's spiritual task as he grows and develops as a Christian person is to make sense out of Christian reality by being part of an adult community; he makes sense out of the Church and its faith by seeing what the adults around him do with it—their love, hope, trust, faith, and faithfulness. Their experience is foundational to their maturing faith-life.[48] This is, of course, the pattern of Jesus who not only taught adults but used peculiarly adult images. This must be our pattern as we plan for a total parish ministry.

This is perhaps one of the most difficult points for parents and pastors to accept since it involves trusting the faith life of the child, his Christian development, to the quality of the spiritual and emotional life of the home. Some religious educators short-circuit the risk by adopting the schooling-instructional model of Christian education. They prefer, like many parents who refuse the sobering conclusions of McCready and Greeley, to isolate specific functions rather than see education as nurture, as a holistic developmental process within the Church as a community.

One hundred and twenty years ago Horace Bushnell, one of the pioneers of American religious education, noted in his *Christian Nurture* (1847) that the child learns by what he sees happening around him; "no truth is really taught by words, or interpreted by intellectual and logical method; truth must be lived into meaning, before it can be truly known."[49] Does this conclusion not find a theological parallel, when, *mutatis mutandi*, Meyendorff writes: "The role of the Church is not, therefore, to impose upon man's mind some truth which otherwise he is unable to perceive, but to make him live and grow in the Spirit, so that he himself may see and experience the Truth."[50] The family for the person, like the Church for all its members, is the matrix of faith development.

Theological Rationale

Several pre-theological and theological principles and themes enable us to understand the family as a spiritual reality. In pursuing these themes I am moving beyond the Biblical affirmations that "it is not good that man should be alone" (Genesis 2:18), "for this reason does a man leave his father and mother and cleave unto a wife" (Genesis 2:24, Matthew 19:5, Mark 10:7), and beyond statements that center on the mystery of Christ and his Church (Ephesians 5:25) and Israel and YHWH (Psalms 25, 51, 90; Isaiah 2; Jeremiah 3).[51]

I would like to deal with three pre-theological frames of reference for the family: (1) the family is the source of trust/love; (2) the family is the source of personhood/identity; and (3) the family is the source of community/intimacy.

In no way do I mean to imply that these are the only possible frames; they are, however, categories which I have found useful in making sense out of the Christian family in theological and sociological terms as foundational to Christian nurture.

The Family as the Matrix of Trust/Love

Growing in faith is a multidimensional phenomenon intertwined with personality developments that condition the very content of the faith experience and the person's perception of that experience; were this not so, then every saint would manifest the same sanctity when, in fact, we can discern as many types of holiness as there are saints. Such is the incarnational modality! In addition, faith is a life-long growth process rooted in trust and love. When we discuss the family, we are discussing not only a child-centered learning/teaching community but a community in which all members grow in faith to degrees and in styles that are characteristics of their age and personality.

Eric Erikson's approach to the emotional development of the human person provides several convenient categories in which to approach Christian nurture.[52] His work focuses on eight stages, or life crises, which are described as necessary to human growth. The resolution of these crises is necessary for continued and healthy emotional development. His four stages or crises through childhood are trust/mistrust, autonomy/shame and doubt, initiative/guilt, and industry/inferiority.[53] For our purpose here, I will consider only the first crisis, that between trust and mistrust. Like any model involving people, this one has its drawbacks and certainly its exceptions, but what remains significant for parents and pastors is the foundational nature of human trust as a pre-theological personality characteristic. The religious dimension for Erikson has its roots in the trusting relationship between the mother and child. The developmental task of infancy is the achievement of basic trust. No human person can be a human person in a healthy and Christian sense if he cannot trust the world, the people around him, and his God. In fact, Peter Berger lists as his first *A Rumor of Angels*, or sign of the transcendent, the underlying order of the universe evident in a mother's caring affirmation to the frightened or hurting child that "It's all right; everything will be fine."[54] Love, like faith, is an active virtue. Ultimately, the ability to trust parents and the ability to trust God exercises the same personality faculty; a healthy personality is integral and whole. The child comes to know through his parents that the world which God has made is reliable and trustworthy. Father Elchaninov writes: "Man enters deeply into the texture of the world through his family alone."[55] Less than this ability is clinically described as neurotic.

Trust is best communicated in family where the relationship is extensive, intensive, and reliable. In the primal relationship of mother-father-infant the child's immediate needs are met. Meeting the child's needs, the root of the trust capacity, is as urgent to him as the mystic's need for a sense of the presence of God. All must stop before the "dirty diaper"! The child can only know God through his parents' touch, whether it fills the stomach, changes the diaper, or fondles the skin. The need for this, though foundational for the infant, does not leave; even as adults "skin hunger" needs must be met. The touch is healing because it conveys love. Incarnational love—"love-with-flesh-on-it"—is real love; love without "touch" is counterfeit. C.S. Lewis has noted:

> We—or at least I—shall not be able to adore God on the highest occasions if we have learned no habit of doing so on the lowest. At best, our faith and reason will tell us that He is adorable, but we shall not have *found* Him so, not have "tested and seen."[55A]

The home is, in principle, the place for children to learn that they can risk failure and still be accepted by their parents; only when children can risk making mistakes can they grow into maturity. The person who is paralyzed by fear, of whatever origin, is the person unable to take the risk and trust God with his life or die for someone else. The family is a place of permissiveness, and I do not mean license, where children can grow in trust and autonomy, which in turn give birth to initiative and industry. A trusting person grows in an environment in which he can risk his ego, but risks are taken only with people whom we have come to trust/love. In fact, even when we speak of growth in faith through modeling, we must be aware that "the young will take seriously what they see taken seriously by others whom they have come to trust. The most important teaching about morality is done by living example."[56] Margaret Sawin, author of the family clustering model of family-centered education, writes that only when persons develop security and trust in themselves can they then have the courage to risk and respond in faith to challenges.[57] Trust is learned in relationship with trustworthy others, not in a school room.

It is not by chance that children raised in homes with severe, excessive, and harsh discipline emerge as untrusting, fearful, and deeply prejudiced persons.[58] Children who cannot trust can only learn to love with great difficulty. Steele and Pollock, for instance, have noted that most of the persons in their study of child abusers were affiliated with some religious group and were mainly from the "strong, rigid, authoritative, 'fundamentalist' type of belief."[59] Rigid, authoritarian parents are generally too insecure to trust responsibility to the child. Fundamentalists, as the Puritan tradition, have a pessimistic view of people.[60] The three-fold distinction in family organization described by Terbert Gans in *The Urban Village: Group and Class in the Life of Italian Americans*[61] is particularly useful. He outlines (1) the adult-centered, parent-dominated family which is run by adults and for adults; (2) the child-centered and laissez-faire permissive family, child-dominated; and finally (3) the authoritative family that places great emphasis on self-development and growth of all of family members, children and adults. This latter pattern has the greatest potential for responsible development; it is characterized (1) by interactive relationships in which the forces exerted by parents and children are in a healthy state of tension and (2) by high levels of responsible, self-directed behavior on the part of children.

The child who experiences only conditional love in the home will find it hard, if not impossible, to love himself, to believe, in turn, that he is loved by God, and, finally, to love others both in a sexual and filial sense. Love is a unity, and the ability to love one's self is immediately related to one's ability to love his God and his neighbor.[62] Jesus knew exactly what he was saying when he urged his hearers to "Love your neighbor as yourself" (Matthew 19:19). For the monastic fathers the movement was simultaneous, and they discussed love in terms of the image of God. In fact, we now learn from contemporary psychologists and common sense that mature love is an expression of self-esteem! Gregory of Nyssa is emphatic on the importance of love to the character of the Image of God in people.[63] If love is absent or enfeebled, then the image is severely altered. The child learns to love in the home by first being loved. He can love because he was first loved (I John 4:10; 4:19). Again, the parents are central— their lifestyles, first, and their words, second. Realistic parenting skills should aim at developing a positive self-concept in a pre-school child, remembering that children behave, believe, and think out their awareness of themselves.

The Family as Matrix of Personhood/Identity

The second major pre-theological theme we find embodied in the Christian understanding of the family is the concept of personhood.[64] The person is a notion fundamental to any understanding of Orthodox Triadology, Christology, or Soteriology. The English word "person" well suits the meaning which came to be applied by the Cappadocians and Chalcedon to "hypostasis," refering basically to the "ego," the agent or locus of self-awareness. The notion of personhood is foundational to *theosis* because God reveals (shares) his life with persons who know who they are as well as who He is. In the theological notion of personhood we find a theological rationale for the family as matrix of pre-theological formation. To this point, Elchaninov writes:

> We can live our entire life—and many in fact do—
> as a pale reflection and copy of someone else. The
> first and primary meaning of life is to be oneself,
> and from this to ascend to the transfiguration of
> oneself into the "image and likeness of God."[65]

In all cultures, the family is the matrix of identity, imprinting its members with a sense of selfhood and personhood, which of necessity encompasses a sense of belonging and a sense of separateness.[66] Here children can achieve a sense of their own identity, their connectedness and separateness.[67] Personhood also has a social dimension. It includes the notion of who "I" am in relationship to other persons. While the discussion of identity is peculiarly well suited to the adolescent person, children normally strive to determine their own identities from the time they are toddlers and use "no" as a means of separating themselves from their parents.

Personhood is fundamental not only because it is the basis of Orthodox theological formulations, but because the content of personhood is the basis of Christian morality. The awareness of self develops with the sense of personhood, and indeed moral and ethical responsibility can be assumed only by those who have a firm notion of their personhood, of themselves as distinct, and, therefore, answerable. The notion of self, however, never occurs as abstraction. It occurs as a notion of self as *something*. A firm notion of personhood develops over a period of years but should be completed sometime in the late teens as an ingredient of adulthood. We do, however, expect that a child of seven can be confessed and can know good from bad. His knowledge of good, bad, acceptable, and unacceptable will depend on his awareness of himself as something, a Christian or a "good boy," for instance. This self-awareness grows out of (1) how adults relate to the child and (2) what they tell the child about who he is; for Christians the second point would include telling the child who God says He is. Sometime in the teen years we expect that a sense of personhood will provide the foundation for a mature notion of human sexuality and sexual interaction. For sex to be responsible, it must be between people who are old enough to have a notion of the personhood of others. Without a clear sense of the personhood of the self and the other we can speak only about exploitation. The emotional and spiritual danger of adolescent sexual activity rests precisely in the fact that adolescents have, in general, not yet established a firm notion of personhood, especially their own. The "other" remains an object.

The Orthodox doctrine of salvation as deification is also based on personhood simply because it is persons who are saved, whose awareness of themselves is transfigured by the grace and spirit of God. God relates to persons (not to natures) as one person to another. Our salvation is rooted in our identifying our personhood with the personhood of Christ, the Logos of God, the subject of the assumed humanity. Man discovers in Jesus Christ more than his true humanity. He discovers his true personhood. *Theosis*, therefore, is rooted in own personhood. Only as person can we encounter Christ! Perhaps, more than in any abstract quality, such as freedom, love, or intelligence, our personhood is the image of God within us.

The family as the matrix of personhood and identity remains central throughout life as the person seeks to use the constancy of the family as a reference point, a place to find validation and plausibility, a stable counterpoise to a society of throw-away relationships. Only the stability of the family can be the matrix of personhood. The historic importance placed on *stabilitas loci* in monastic development, east and west, speaks to the same spiritual issue. In this context, we can more fully understand the sacramental nature of the family; it is such, however, only when we can discern in its functioning an element of connectedness between its real experience, the *is*, and the mystery of the union of Christ and His Church, the *ought*. Erikson notes, with sobering seriousness, that "the most deadly of all possible sins is the mutilation of the child's spirit."[68] Every family must aim for congruency!

As I have said elsewhere, the family's sense of its own spiritual heritage and of where it belongs has much to say to the child's growing sense of who he is and where he belongs. Any pastoral ministry must aim at increasing the family's sense of its connectedness with the Church, a sense of heritage, belief and celebration. Humanity is by nature *homo festivus*; it is through ritual and celebration that every group manifests its experience of reality. The child's identity, for instance, as an Orthodox, first develops around practices, not beliefs. He knows he belongs to a particular community by the rituals he shares with that community. What it is to be Orthodox is not defined by belief, but by practice. It is by "practice" that he develops a distinct corporate identity.[69] Celebrations are by their nature communal and community-forming events; they tie us together in a shared experience which is at once horizontal, those we are living with, and vertical, those that have come before us and will come after.[70] These are essential to a child's sense of belonging as well as to adults' memories of a sense of belonging. It is ritual and celebration that remain in the life of the Christian person the element of connectedness which overcomes the alienation so characteristic of societies in rapid change. Dostoevsky, with insight we mistakenly associate only with clinical therapy, put the following in Alyosha Karamazov's words:

> You must know that there is nothing higher and stronger and more wholesome and good for life in the future than some good memory, especially a memory of childhood, of home. People talk to you a great deal about your education, but some good sacred memory, preserved from childhood, is perhaps the best education. If a man carries many such memories with him into life, he is safe to the end of his days, and if one has only one good memory left in one's heart, even that may sometime be the means of saving us.[71]

The family must be a teacher of celebration. Heim writes:

> On no account should the family fail to seize every opportunity of using traditional celebrations, symbols and play so as to create high points in family life, to provide an atmosphere of intimacy, belonging, and trust and to bring order and meaning...to an otherwise threatening chaos.[72]

Through celebrating our common salvation, adults and children alike make the content their own and come to see themselves in terms of those celebrations. A family which has no liturgy and no celebration has no meaning; its children are rootless and their personhood without focus.

The Family as the Matrix of Intimacy/Community

The two previous categories, trust/love and personhood/ identity, are intimately related to the third, intimacy/ community.

The New Testament does not give attention to intimacy in marriage, except, of all places, in the letter of St Paul to the Ephesians where he compares marriage to the relationship between Christ and His Church (Ephesians 5:25); by extrapolation to the Old Testament the same intimacy, taken from the image of Israel's relationships with YHWH, appears in the Song of Songs and the Psalms. Intimacy is one of the functions of marriage, yet, ethically, it is not an exclusive function; that is, it is not intimacy in the family community as opposed to intimacy in the neighborhood or the parish; it is intimacy in the family which is the basis for intimacy outside the family. The family is not sufficient to this, and it is a mistake to believe that the nuclear family by itself can maintain intimacy. Hence, any family-life or family-centered catechesis must involve as much of the community as possible—liturgy, service, social, and educational activities. The Church, essentially a conservative institution, must continue to provide elements of constancy (=world maintenance) in a society which offers no prospect of social or technical plateauing and, consequently, minimal stability. World maintenance is important not simply because it is the Church's nature, but because the disruption of the family, for example, has a profound effect on the emotional and spiritual growth of the people of the Church. Divorce, for instance, is a social issue which is at once spiritual. One author notes:

> I am persuaded that in the technobureaucratic city
> of most present day forms of government the fam-
> ily remains one of the few warm currents of
> humanity. If we allow this fundamental social

material to decay, neither reform, nor revolution,
nor the status quo will be possible, because the
most basic human element will be absent.[73]

The family is the child's first community in which he experiences intimacy, characterized best by security, warmth, and love. Without experiencing intimacy in this primal community, he will probably not find expression for his growing personhood and sense of personhood. In the intimacy that characterizes communal life, the child and the adult experience the personhood of others and self; human interaction, based on consistency and commitment, feeds the growing sense of identity. Hence, one of the dilemmas with day care—the care of children by "no one in particular" or "casual" communitites—is the exclusion of the attachment necessary for intimacy as "prerequisite for human existence."[74] The intimacy of the family as community provides the foundation for meeting the "outside" world and determines whether or not children will find it exciting and wonder-filled or hostile and terror-filled. In this sense the family lays the foundation for its own annihilation as children grow trustingly into the world outside of the family, into the parish, into the school, into the neighborhood. It is also this factor which places the Christian family at the root of social service and the struggle for justice. Indeed, if the family does not open the child to the world as a wonder-filled object of service, it has failed. Self-giving love, whose ultimate objective is the service of God's world, is learned in the warmth of the home.

Developmentally, children are ready for pre-ethical thinking between the ages of five and seven, when they are ready for social(=mutual) play. Before five, children tend not to play together; even though with one another, they tend to play alone or in parallel.[75] Community is the opposite of *privatism* or the preoccupation with the self or an object (television or computer, for instance). Certain activities encourage privatism and inhibit moral development.[76] At around seven, children begin to play with each other and make rules; they begin to be able to project themselves mentally into different roles and perceive conflicts from different perspectives. This is referred to as role transfer, moral imagination, or role projection. The process is much more complicated, but the words of Atticus in *To Kill A Mockingbird*, make the point well enough:

> "First of all," he said, "if you can learn a simple trick, Scout, you'll get along a lot better with all kinds of folks. You never really understand a person until you consider things from his point of view—" "Sir?"
> "—until you climb into his skin and walk around in it."[77]

I am not suggesting that this is Christian morality; I am suggesting that the ability to think morally and empathetically cannot develop without the ability to self-project; the development of projection is directly related to living in a community and, particularly in the case of young children, learning to play.

We can expect Christian and ethical behavior from a person whose mental development allows it, to the extent that he perceives himself as a Christian. This self-awareness derives from the family in two senses; first, in the sense that the family lays the foundation for a primitive type of morality does not involve the freedom of which the child is not yet capable. Inasmuch as the family is essentially community and not an autocracy, the child is permitted to grow out of this heteronomous stage as the parents increasingly share leadership and responsibility.[79] In the community of family the child can take risks in experimenting with his behavior as he grows into an autonomy in which his behavior is governed from within. The development of autonomous morality is encouraged only through human interaction and for the school-age child most notably, again, in situations of play.

Children need a community, but not one structured on power and coercion, to develop this ability to think ethically.[80] Before this, parents can "force" ethical behavior, such as sharing a toy, but they have not produced ethical thinking. Sharing is not a self-evident virtue for the infant or early child; it is a type of "death" or "theft." Reciprocity makes no sense to a youngster until he can project himself into another's role. The initial stages of moral development depends upon a community and the interaction within that community. This interaction must become increasingly mutual as the child matures chronologically and outgrows his infantile egocentrism. It is not by accident that about the age of seven the child begins to go to confession and to take interest in his community outside of the immediate nuclear family.[81]

Finally, and more specifically, Christianity, as I have said before, is not an adult's religion and the child must make sense out of it by seeing what the faithful and trusted adults around him are doing with it. C. Ellis Nelson, a highly respected religious educator, writes:

> My thesis is that faith is communicated by a community of believers and that the meaning of faith is developed by its members out of their history, by their interaction with each other, and in relationship to events that take place in their lives.[82].

The child discovers what it is to be a Christian by being told what it means, but primarily by experiencing the reality of the living community, whether parish or family.

What sociologists seem to have missed in the socialization model of Christian development is the simple reality that whatever our belief system, our commitment to that system tends to be directly proportional to the quality, size, and extent of the community sharing it. It is not only the strength, quality, and consistency of the family's belief and value structures that influence a child; it is also the plausibility of those structures created by the size and frequency of contact with the parish community which affects the strength of the child's early commitment to a particular set of beliefs.[83]

Whatever the theory of moral development, religious sociologists such as Uri Bronfenbrenner have noted that the family as an immediate influence on the youths' moral standards is losing out to the peer group, and he sees this as a result of industrialization and its fragmentation of the family.[84] If this is true, it is by default; the Christian family is still the place where the child learns who he is and where he belongs. The family (1) is the source of security, sense of self, and sense of belonging, and (2) enables the child to know who he is as a Christian. It is this two-fold development which is the basis for Christian ethics. Only in a secondary sense does the moral education within the family consist of the presentation of "rules."

The Church must encourage and develop lateral relationships. The nuclear family constitutes a limited community. As one writer has noted: "The paradox is that the parents are too close, exclusive, 'caring,' and ubiquitous emotionally."[85] By definition, the nuclear family is stripped down and usually consists of a mother, a father, and one or two children. This small family unit creates problems unknown to the extended family. The power and influence of the peer group is correspondingly exaggerated. The nuclear family is crowded with emotions that can find no release; in the extended family there was always a grandparent, aunt, or uncle nearby to provide a safety valve for the children or the parents. If extended families do not or cannot exist due to mobility and distance, then the Church can and should attempt to provide this extended family by artificially creating an affective or faith circle. Alvin Toffler, in his *The Third Wave*,[86] holds out great hope for alternate family forms as the nuclear family collapses and continues only as one among numerous options for communal living.[87]

The Church has tended to encourage diversified lateral relationships to expand the community and has itself provided for the "affective circle" characteristic of Toffler's First Wave family. This is true in the canonical incest taboos and spiritual relationships as well as in the tradition of the confessor (the *geron* or *staretz*); in *The Brothers Karamazov*, it is Father Zosima who keeps the Karamazov family "open" to the outside world, keeps it from being consumed by its own internal squabbles. The godfather and the godmother have played the same role. I believe that in the context of the "affective circle" we can make sense out of the incest taboos unrelated to blood or gene pools.[88]

Conclusions

We have suggested some theological foundations for the Christian family as the primal educator, not in terms of didactic techniques, but in terms of pre-theological formation. In the family the child grows in trust and love, in personhood and identity, and in his sense of intimacy and community. These human realities are the incarnational context in which parents share in God's work of creating free men and women who are open to his love and his grace. These then are both the basis and goal for a family-centered and family-life educational ministry.

One need be neither sociologist nor pastor to know that the family is in trouble.[89] Rapid social changes are afoot, and the western, technological, capitalist world seems caught in a spiral of movement which knows no plateau as it moves toward the demassed society of Alvin Toffler's *Third Wave* world.[90] Rapid social change corrodes any human relationship, but particularly the family. In the last two to three hundred years the family has, in fact, been one of the few social constants; Gabriel Moran has written that the "family is the center of concern because it has not collapsed and we can see it sagging under the weight of the communal burden."[91] The family has changed little over the centuries and there is little likelihood it will change in the future. One futurist has noted, however, that while this might be the case, more and more people are choosing to live outside of the traditional family unit. This will create problems as more people find themselves in essentially unstable social relationships. The Church is called upon to provide more of the support that the extended family used to provide

More conscientious Christian parenting begins with the discovery of the foundations of Christian family life and parenting; the second step is to consciously decide what we want to do to enable the family to conform to those foundations; the third step is to determine the methods needed to achieve the goals decided upon.

Several guidelines are in order. From a systems approach to family life and family-centered catechesis, we know that nothing happens to people in vacuums. The family must be treated as a unit and education programs designed for groupings of these units; the single learner concept is bankrupt because people do not live, learn, or develop alone. Family education must not be allowed to become a mask for adult education or a guise for teaching children. In addition, we must understand that cognitive learning has been given priority over affective learning because it is easier to accomplish and to evaluate. It, however, must not dominate family-life or family-centered catechetical programs.

Neither, however, can it be ignored. Hence, we can speak of family-life and family-centered educational ministries.[92]

If we do not maintain the home as the primary, though not exclusive, responsibility for the nuture of its children, then we are violating the theology we are so fond of touting. We will have a faith in one space and a family in another with no meaningful interaction; there will be no flesh on our theology, and theology without flesh is dead and deadly to its practitioners.

Chapter 3 Footnotes

[1]Hermas, *The Pastor*, in *Ante-Nicene Fathers*, Vol. 2 (New York: C. Scribners, 1926), 48, 51.

[2]Justin Martyr, *Apologies*, in *Ante-Nicene Fathers*, Vol. 1 (New York: C. Scribners, 1926), 156.

[3]*Nicene and Post-Nicene Fathers,* Second Series, Vol. 14 (Grand Rapids, MI: Eerdmans, n.d.), 93, 95.

[4]*Ibid.*, 98. The following canon, #16, also condemned children who, under the same pretext, neglected their parents. Ignatius of Antioch takes up the same theme: "Tell my sisters to love the Lord and be content with their husbands in the flesh and the spirit. In like manner, charge my brothers in the name of Jesus Christ to love their wives, as the Lord loved the Church." See Epistle to Polycarp, 5 in *Ante-Nicene Fathers*, Vol. 1 (New York: C. Scribners, 1926), 95.

[5]See for an example of this tendency to idealize marriage, John Meyendorff, *Marriage, An Orthodox Perspective*, (Crestwood, NY: SVS Press, 1970), 57-58.

[6]*Ibid.*, 21.

[7]St John Chrysostom, "Homily 20 on Ephesians," in *Nicene and Post Nicene Fathers*, Second Series, Vol. 13 (Grand Rapids, MI: Eerdmans, 1956), 143-152, at 145.

[8]Meyendorff, *op.cit.*, 20.

[9]Meyendorff, *op. cit.*, and Demetrios Constantelos, *Marriage, Sexuality, and Celibacy: A Greek Orthodox Perspective* (Minneapolis: Light and Life Publishing Company, 1965). For an historical treatment of the family, see Jean Remy, "The Family: Contemporary Models and Historical Perspectives" in Andrew Greeley (ed.), *The Family in Crisis Or in Transition* (New York: Seabury Press, 1979), 3-14; see also the more substantial and more readable survey of Christian marriage by Roland H. Bainton, *Sex, Love, and Marriage* (Glascow: Fontana Books, 1957). Moran, *Education Toward Adulthood*, (New York: Paulist Press, 1979), chapter 5, offers a brief history of the family and the assurance that it will survive as the only viable option for nurturing children. In addition, see the analysis of childhood and childrearing practices from the middle ages to the modern period in Winn, *op.cit.*, 87-107.

[10]Samuel Natale, "A Family Systems Approach to Religious Education and Development," *Religious Education*, 74 (May/June, 1979), 246.

[11]See C. Ellis Nelson, *Where Faith Begins* (New York: Seabury Press, 1976); John H. Westerhoff, III, *Will Our Children Have Faith?* (New York: Seabury Press, 1976); and Berard Marthaler, "Socialization as a Mode for Catechesis," in P. O'Hare, *Foundations of Religious Education* (New York: Paulist Press, 1978), 64-92; and John L. Boojamra, "Socialization as an Historical Model for Christian Integration," *St. Vladimir's Theological Quarterly*, 25 (1981), 219-237.

[12]See Constantelos, *op.cit.*, 51-52; and Meyendorff, *op.cit.*, 23-27.

[13]It should be noted that I am working with a rather narrow definition in the context of contemporary Christian educators, such as Gabriel Moran and Dolores Curran, who operate from a sociological perspective. During the past two decades different forms of "families" have arisen so that sociologists have difficulty using the term scientifically; there is a tendency to refer to any person living in any relationship with another, usually in one household, as a family.

Margaret Sawin, the respected American Baptist founder of the Family Cluster Model of education, illustrates this confusion in definition when, for example, she speaks of "homosexual families"; see Margaret Sawin, "Community and Family: Growing in Faith Through Family Clusters," in Maria Harris (ed.), *Parish Religious Education* (New York: Paulist Press, 1978), 41-55, at 50; and Gabriel Moran, "Community and Family: The Way We Are: Communal Forms and Church Response," in *ibid.*, 25-40, at 34, emphatically notes: "This love [the homophile relationship] is especially challenging to the classification of people as married or single because lovers are neither isolated individuals nor are they getting together to have children." Their definitions are so broad and all inclusive as to be virtually useless for my purposes inasmuch as they are so radically out of keeping with Orthodox tradition. It is my concern that we as a Church in North America become aware of our theology, tradition, and customs in keeping with those traditions so that we can attempt to shape the future practively rather than reactively. This problem of definition is symptomatic of the fact that the family is not certain what its purpose or function is. Not only is there a Freudian-induced uncertainty described recently by Marie Winn, *Children Without Childhood*, (New York: Pantheon Books, 1981), 98-99, but the phenomenon of the "executive parent" described by Kenneth Keniston, *All Our Children* (New York: Harcourt, Brace, Jovanovich, 1977), 12-22, as the parent dependent on other agencies to manage his children, including Christian education. Keniston claims that parents have not abdicated their functions as most of those function have been removed by agencies.

[14]Jean B. Elstain, "Feminism and Family," *American Educator*, 7 (Summer, 1983), 20-25 at 23. Elstain offers an analysis of the negative relationship of feminism to the family which is typical of the more traditionalist approach of the American Federation of Teachers. See John Chrysostom, "Homily 20" in *op.cit.*, 149, on the destructive nature of the word *mine*. Also see, C.S. Lewis, *The Screwtape Letters* (New York: Macmillan, 1960), 106-110.

[15]Sidney Callahan, *Family Religious Education* (Washington, D.C.: National Conference of Diocesan Directors of Religious Education, 1974), 20.

[16]James Goldman, *The Lion In Winter* (New York: Random House, 1966), 91.

[17]Meyendorff, *op.cit.*, 59-60, also notes this function of monasticism.

[18]Basil of Caesarea, "Regulae fusius tractatae," Interrogatio 7 in J.P. Migne, *Patrologiae Graecae, Cursus Completus, Series Graecia*, Vol. 31 (1885), col. 928-929.

[19]Clement of Alexandria, Stromata, Book I, 3, translated by J.E.L. Oulton and H. Chatwich (Library of Christian Classics II, Philadelphia: Westminster Press, 1954), 41-42. In general however Clement was negative on sexual intercourse, even in the condition of marriage; see George W. Forrell, *History of Christian Ethics* (Minneapolis: Augsburg, 1979), 61-88.

[20]*Ibid.*, 77.

[21]John H. Westerhoff, III, *Will Our Children Have Faith?* (New York: Seabury Press, 1976), 23, for example. Westerhoff's book has received good review elsewhere by this author. With few exceptions, most Orthodox will feel comfortable with Westerhoff's approach: Faith can be inspired within a community of faith, but it cannot be given to one person by another. Faith is expressed, transformed, and made meaningful by persons sharing their faith in an historical, tradition-bearing community of faith.

[22]*Ibid.*, 22.

[23]John L. Boojamra, "Socialization as a Historical Model for Christian Integration," *St. Vladimir's Theological Quarterly*, 25 (1981), 219-239.

[24]Henri I Marrou, *A History of Education in Antiquity*, translated by George Lambe (New York: Sheed and Ward, 1956), 314; see also Lukas Vischer "Introduction into the Life of Faith in the Early Church," *RISK*, 2 (1st quarter, 1966), 40-46. There tended to be a central role for the family as is evident in the Lecture of St John Chrysostom, *On Vainglory and How Parents Should Bring Up Their Children*, translated by M.L.W. Laistner, *Christianity and Pagan Culture* (Ithaca: n.p., 1951), as the matrix of education; the role of the father was particularly significant.

[25]See John L. Boojamra, *Baptism, the Way to Life* (Englewood, NJ: Department of Christian Education, 1979), for an example of a pre-baptismal program for parents, highlighting their responsibilities for the faith of the child. For a Roman Catholic strong statement on this, see Ferdinand Klosterman, "Decree on the Apostolate of the Laity," in *Commentary on the Documents of Vatican II* (New York: Herder and Herder, 1969), 111:339.

[26]M. Sawin, *op.cit.*, 42.

[27]William McCready, "The Family and Socialization," in Andrew Greeley, *"The Family in Crisis or in Transition* (New York: Seabury Press, 1979), 27.

[28]Andrew Greeley, *The New Agenda* (New York: Doubleday Image, 1975), 244.

[29]Andrew M. McCready, and Peter H. Rossi, *The Education of Catholic Americans*, (Garden City, NY: Anchor Books, 1968), 116.

[30]Raymond Potvin, Dean Hoge, and Hart Nelson, *Religion and American Youth, With Emphasis on Catholic Adolescents and Young Adults* (Washington, D.C.; Boys Town Center for the Study of Youth Development, n.d.), 21.

[31]John Meyendorff, *Living Tradition* (Crestwood, NY: SVS Press, 1978), 38.

[32]Elchaninov, *Diary of a Russian Priest* (London: Faber and Faber, 1967), 46.

[33]Meyendorff, *Marriage*, 15.

[34]Elchaninov, *op.cit.*, 46.

[35]Meyendorff, *Marriage*, 58-59. See also the fascinating social, economic, and political projections in Alvin Toffler, *The Third Wave* (New York: William Morrow, Co., 1980), 118. Systems thinking stresses the holistic rather than the fragmented perspective on situations and issues. It made its way out of the labs, the traditional locus of scientific specification, in the mid 1950's and since then its language has been employed by sociologists and philosophers. One of the most obvious manifestations of this type of thinking is the ecological movement which tends to see reality in terms of "webs." Toffler traces a great deal of social disjointedness to Cartesian emphasis on the analysis of components at the expense of context.

[36]Minuchin, *Families and Family Therapy* (Cambridge, Harvard University Press, 1974), 133.

[37]Samuel Natale, "Family Therapist: An Emerging Role for Ministry," Gloria Durka and Joanmarie Smith (eds.), *Family Ministry*, (Minneapolis: Winston Press, 1980), 130-140, at 131.

[38]For an analysis from a Roman Catholic perspective see Dolores Curran, "Family Ministry and the Parish: Barriers and Visions," in Durka and Smith, *op.cit.*, 2-23.

[39]See Boojamra, "Socialization," 220-221.

[40]John Elias, "The Christian Family as Moral Educator," in Durka and Smith, *op.cit.*, 37.

[41]See for example, Lucie Barber, John Hiltz, and Louise Skoch, "Ministry to Parents of the Little Child," *Religious Education*, 74 (May/June, 1974), 263-269, at 264.

[42]Barber, *op.cit.*, 264.

[43]William McCready, "The Family and Socialization," in Andrew Greeley, *The Family*, 26-34 at 26-27.

[44]*Ibid.*, 33.

[45]Gabriel Moran, "The Professions and the Family," in Durka and Smith, *op. cit.*, 127. Also on the new centrality accorded the father in the family structure, see Maureen Green, *Fathering* (New York: McGraw-Hill Books, 1977); Eliot Daley, *Father Feeling* (New York: William Morrow, 1978); and Harold Isaacs, "Rediscovering Fathers," *American Educator*, 7 (Fall, 1983), 23-25.

[46]Andrew Greeley, *Agenda*, 242. See also Andrew Greeley, William McCready, and K. McCourt, *The Catholic School in a Declining Church* (Kansas City: Sheed and Ward, 1976), for a complete discussion of the statistical findings of the National Opinion Research Center.

[47]It is not inappropriate for an Orthodox parish to focus its educational energies on education for *role fulfillment*, examining various relationships within a family system from a scriptural, traditional, and societal perspective. In general, people are highly motivated to fulfill their roles more effectively.

[48]Westerhoff, *Will Our Children*, 92.

[49]Horace Bushnell, *Christian Nurture* (reprint, New Haven: Yale University Press, 1947), 204; Bushnell, an early nineteenth-century liberal, was prepared to admit the young child to the full worship of the church, even to holy communion; *ibid.*, 63. For an excellent, albeit brief, treatment of *Christian Nurture*, see Randolph C. Miller, "Bushnell, the Family and Children," in *Religious Education*, 74 (May/June, 1979), 254-262.

[50]Meyendorff, *Tradition*, 41; italics are the author's.

[51]On the place of Ephesians 5:25 in Byzantine Christian tradition, see Meyendorff, *Byzantine Theology* (New York: Fordham University Press, 1974), 196-199.

⁵²John Elias, *Psychology and Religious Education* (Bethlehem, PA: Catechetical Communications, 1975), 35-36. For a brilliant application of his theories to religious development, see Erik Erikson, *Young Man Luther* (New York; Norton, 1958).

⁵³Erik Erikson, *Childhood and Society* (New York: Norton, 1950), 65ff. Understanding Erikson's crises as well as Piaget's stages enables teachers, parents, and pastors to understand the limitations as well as the opportunitites offered by each period; see T. Litz, "The Family as the Developmental Setting," in E.J. Anthony *et. al.*, *The Child in His Family* (New York: John Wiley and Sons, 1970), 20.

⁵⁴Peter Berger, *A Rumor of Angels* (New York: Doubleday, 1969), 69.

⁵⁵Elchaninov, *op.cit.*, 46.

⁵⁵ᴬC.S. Lewis, *Letters to Malcolm: Chiefly on Prayer* (New York: A Harvest Book, 1964), 91.

⁵⁶William Bennet and Edwin Delatre, "A Moral Education," *American Educator*, 6 (Summer, 1982), 6-9, at 6.

⁵⁷Margaret Sawin, "Community and Family: Growing in Faith Through Family Clusters," in Maria Harris (ed.), *Parish Religious Education* (New York: Paulist Press, 1978), 43.

⁵⁸See the old but still very valuable work of Gordon Allport, *The Nature of Prejudice* (Garden City, NY: Doubleday Anchor Books, 1951).

⁵⁹See C. Pollock and B. Steele, "A Psychiatric Study of Parents who Abuse Infants and Small Children," quoted in Kathryn Neufield, "Child Rearing, Religion, and Abusive Parents," *Religious Education*, 74 (May/June, 1979), 234-244, at 236. Certain studies indicate, for instance, that many fundamentalist Christian believers have personality profiles similar to child abusers. Many believe that children are innately depraved. Such was the basis for the generally negative view of childhood play among American Puritans. See Janet Fishburn, "The Family as Means of Grace in American Theology," *Religious Education*, 78 (Winter, 1983), 90-102, especially at 93-94. On the importance of play to emotional development, see Winn, *op.cit.*, 77-83. Play is an area whose liturgical and ethical implications would provide a fruitful area of study for an Orthodox student. Also Merton Stromenn, *Five Cries of Youth* (New York: Harper & Row, 1979), 77.

⁶⁰See L.D. Streiber and B.S. Strober, "Religion and the New Majority." On violence towards children in America see D.G. Gill, *Violence Against Children* (Cambridge: Harvard University Press, 1970).

⁶¹Herbert Gans, *The Urban Villagers: Group and Class in the Life of Italian Americans* (New York: Free Press, 1962) chapter 5. Gans distinguished three manners of dealing with authority in the family. The Family as locus of values must demonstrate a clear sense of its own authority. Authority has traditionally resided in the father; a good argument can be made for the case that it must reside in one person if authority is not to be an impersonal rather than an interpersonal force. Once authority is *personal*, it can be shared, as with the siblings as they mature into responsibility. See Moran, "Professions," in Durka and Smith, *op.cit.*, 109. For Bushnell, the family is the place of God-given authority; see Bushnell, *op.cit.*, 272, and Miller, *op.cit.*, 260-261.

[62]I am not using self-love in the patristic sense of *philautis*; see J.L. Boojamra, "Original Sin According to St. Maximus the Confessor," *St Vladimir's Theological Quarterly*, 20 (1976), 19-30. It is used here in the sense of the love of neighbor as self as in Matthew 19:19, 22:39, and Mark 12:31, 33.

[63]Gregory of Nyssa, *De Hominis Opificio*, in J.P. Migne, *Patrologiae Graecae, Cursus Completus*, Series Graeca, Vol. 44, col. 137. See also, St Basil the Great, *op.cit.*, 908.

[64]It is this author's belief that the peculiar Orthodox contribution to family-life ministry, family-centered catechesis, and theological reflection on the family is the foundational theological reality of personhood.

[65]Elchaninov, *op.cit.*, 82.

[66]S. Minuchin, *op.cit.*, 47.

[67]Samuel Natale, *Pastoral Counseling* (New York: Paulist Press, 1977), 71.

[68]Erikson, *Childhood*, 250.

[69]Robert L. Browing, "Festivity—From a Protestant Perspective," *Religious Education*, 73 (May/June 1980), 273-281, at 273. For further reference see Erik Erikson, *Toys and Reasons: Stages in the Ritualization of Life* (New York: Norton, 1977).

[70]See Roger D. Abrahmas, "Celebrations Mark Great Occasions the World Around," *Smithsonian*, 108-116, at 112. In spite of the mobility of Americans, the author notes correctly that emotional stability is maintained by sharing old festivals with new people in new places.

[71]Fyodor Dostoevsky, *The Brothers Karamazov*, translated by Constance Garnet. (The Great Books of the Western World, #52; Chicago: William Benton, 1952), 411.

[72]Walter Heim, "Religious Practice Within the Family: A Contribution to the Theology of Intimate Belonging in the Light of Popular Beliefs and Customs in the Past," in Greeley, *Family*, 82-88, at 87.

[73]Jacques Grand-Maison, "The Modern Family: Locus of Resistance or Agency of Change?" in Andrew Greeley, *Family*, 47-60, at 58.

[74]C. Ellis Nelson, *Where Faith Begins* (Philadelphia: John Knox Press, 1967), 10; at the same time that we are becoming aware of the importance of community for personal emotional development and stability, we are experiencing a radical decline in the family as community as more and more mothers of school-age children work, leaving fewer significant adults with whom the child is able to interact. At the same time that the number of elderly is increasing, the number actually living with family members has decreased significantly. For similar statistics see, Urie Brofenbrenner, *The Calamitous Decline of the American Family*, (Washington, D.C.: U.S. Office of Education, 1976). See also Mary Durkin, "Intimacy and Marriage: Continuing Mystery of Christ and the Church," in Greeley, *The Family*, 74-81, at 76.

[75]See Lawrence Kohlberg, Stages of Moral Development as a Basis for Moral Education," in C.H. Beck et al, *Moral Education: Interdisciplinary Approaches* (Toronto: University of Toronto, 1971), 86-88.

[76]Kohlberg has noted the danger of privatism in an interview in *The New York Times* emphasizing its negative implications for moral development of children; F.M. Hechingerr, "Can Morality be Taught?", *New York Times*, March 6, 1979, c1, c4.

[77]Harper Lee, *To Kill A Mockingbird*, (New York: Harper and Row, 1960).

[78]Ronald Duska and Mariellen Whelan, *Moral Development: A Guide to Piaget and Kohlberg* (New York: Paulist Press), 7-11.

[79]*Ibid.*, 13-15; see also John Elias, "The Christian Family as Moral Educator," in Durka and Smith, *op.cit.*, 35-55, at 47.

[80]Duska and Whelan, *op.cit.*, 112-113.

[81]Kohlberg's description of stages three and four in his schema of moral development emphasizes the social nature, focusing on group values and the meeting of group (nation, family, church, friends) expectations. Lawrence Kohlberg, "Stages of Moral Development and Moral Education," in Brenda Munsey (ed.), *Moral Development, Oral Education, and Kohlberg* (Birmingham, AL: Religious Education Press, 1980), 15-100, at 91-92. See Duska and Whelan, *op.cit.*, 42-79 for an excellent introduction to Kohlberg's stages.

[82]C. Ellis Nelson, *Where Faith Begins* (Richmond, VA: John Knox Press, 1967), 10. It is because faith is communicated by the community that a strong argument can and should be made for all religious education beginning with adults. Also C. Ellis Nelson, "Our Oldest Problem," in Padraic O'Hare (ed.), *Transformation and Tradition in Religious Education* (Birmingham, AL: Religious Education Press, 1979), 69.

[83]Peter Berger, *op.cit.*, 34-35: "We obtain our notions about the world originally from human beings, and these notions continue to be plausible to us in a very large measure because others continue to affirm them."

[84]Urie Bronfenbrenner, "The Role of Age, Sex, Class and Culture in Studies of Moral Development," *Religious Education*, 47 (1952), 3-17.

[85]Grand-Maison, *op.cit.*, 53.

[86]Alvin Toffler, *The Third Wave* (New York: William Morrow and Company, 1980), 227: "The coming of the Third Wave, of course, does not mean the end of the nuclear family anymore than the coming of the Second Wave meant the end of the extended family. In means, rather, that the nuclear family can no longer serve as the ideal model for society," Orthodox will hardly be able to mourn its passing!! But what will replace it and how will the various possibilities conform to Orthodox definitions or experience of what a family is?

[87]Moran, *op.cit.*, 82-83.

[88]For instance see Canon 23 of St. Basil (*Nicene and Post-Nicene Fathers*, vol. 14, 606), which states "that a man ought not to marry two sisters [serially], nor a woman two brothers; that he who marries his brother's wife, be not admitted until he dismisses her." Again Canon 21 of I Nicea speaks of incestuous marriages as contrary to the law of spiritual relation; the canon applied to godparents and prescribed a twenty year penance; (*ibid.*, 47). Again, Canon 23 of the same council speaks of prohibited marriages between spiritual brothers and sisters (*ibid.*); Canon 53 of the Quinisext Council forbids marriage of godparents with a widowed parent of their godchild (*ibid.*, 390). The obvious effect, regardless of the intent at a given time and place, of these canons was the extension of the affective community.

[89]That the family and marriage is in trouble can hardly be doubted and can easily be demonstrated by no more than a reference to the steep rise in the rate of divorce and the absolute numbers of divorces. In addition there are well over a million runaways a year and a three-fold increase in suicide between the ages of fifteen and nineteen since 1956; see Edward Wynn, "Adolescent Alienation and Youth Policy," *Teachers' College Record*, 78 (September, 1976), 23-40.

[90]Toffler, *op.cit.*, 230-235.

[91]Moran, *Education Toward*, 93.

[92]See Sandra DeGidio, *Sharing Faith in the Family: A Guide to Ritual and Catechesis* (West Mystic, CT: Twenty-Third Publications, 1980); DeGidio lists family ministry programs centering on peer group, family learning teams, family clusters, liturgical and sacramental activities. DeGidio's is a good introduction to these various programming formats and their relative success.

CHAPTER 4

Foundations in Moral Development

In spite of much contemporary discussion of values and morality in North America,[1] we find ourselves living without a moral consensus. To move toward such a consensus we must first consider how morality and values develop.

The moral development of people, in general, and children, in particular, can be treated from a variety of perspectives. It may be approached from the perspective of moral attitudes, moral cognition, or moral behavior. It may also be approached by focusing on the various current patterns of moral development—behavioral, psychoanalytical, and developmental—in order to critique these in the light of practical Christian experience. The subject also may be considered historically in the patterns and the content evident in the normative patristic writers of the Church.[2] Finally, the Christian writer must make sense out of the three approaches by attempting an integrated perspective, drawing some useful practical conclusions about how to apply these approaches, categorical or methodological, to the family and to learning situations.

Moral development can be broken down into tractable, discussable units, which cannot be separated from one another in a theological perspective, but, nonetheless, are distinguishable logically and pedagogically. In this chapter I shall discuss morality from the behavioral, psychoanalytical, and developmental perspectives and then focus on the cognitive-developmental model as convenient for us Christians to apply to moral education in the home and the parish community. The schema to be used is the relatively controversial model of Lawrence Kohlberg,[3] who along with Jean Piaget has been influential in establishing the themes as well as categories in which Christian educators can work.[4] In addition, I will draw on Erik Erikson to place the discussion in a more useful Christian setting. Focusing on the developmentalists in both their positive and negative implications will enable us to narrow the discussion of moral education down to its cognitive moral element.[5]

It does not take much to reach the conclusion that children are born neither moral nor religious, but rather with the capacity to learn and to feel. The Christian Fathers assumed that development, process, or some form of growth was necessary for personhood. Clement of Alexandria early observed that:

> For it is not by nature, but by learning that people become noble and good, as people also become physicians and pilots.[6]

In general it is safe to conclude that morality develops by 1) the way we treat children, 2) the things we tell them that God says about them, 3) how they develop naturally, and 4) what they see from those whom they trust. How people come to look at themselves depends on a combination of all four factors. The possibility of heightening moral reasoning skills among children and adults is a legitimate goal of the Christian education enterprise.

But approaching morality without approaching content is difficult. It is the paradox of the rich young man: "If you will

be perfect, give what you have to the poor and follow me"
(Matthew 22:37-39). What is perfection? What does it mean
to "follow"? "What constitutes the ethical person?" "What is
the faithful person?" is perhaps a more appropriate question.
The connection between faith as a relationship and ethical
behavior was assumed; it was not analyzed. Early morality
was issue-centered or patterned.[7] In addition it was intuited
that spirituality and morality were the same psychological
thrust; the quality of the relationship with God is immediately related to the quality of the relationship with the
neighbor. Christian morality is therefore relational; it must
be worked out, lived, and developed *in context*. Being both
relational and contextual, Christian morality has two logical
foci, God and the neighbor.

The discussion is further complicated since we are speaking not of a once-and-for-all phenomenon, but of a multidimensional process of personality formation and personality
characteristics. Morality is not *sui generis*; it exists as part of
the personal and spiritual development.

As I have already noted in an earlier chapter of this book,
the learning of Christian categories, including morality, uses
the same faculties as learning other skills and information.[8]
When we discuss the person and personhood, we are in the
realm of mystery, whose ultimate goal we can claim with St
Paul is the maturing to the stature and fullness of Christ
(Ephesians 4:13). There can in the mystery of personhood
be no simple application of principles. Pastoral and pedagogical experience demands that moral development be
treated as an art rather than a precise profession. Certainly,
Gregory of Nazianzus realized this:

> For the guiding of man, the most variable and
> manifest of creatures, seems to me in very deed to
> be the art of arts and science of sciences.[9]

When I discuss morality as moral thinking capacity, I am

talking about it in terms of *windows* for grace; without this, morality is reduced to mere conformity to a set of wills. The freedom, however, to choose among alternatives is an approach inadequate to the patristic understanding of freedom, which includes action in accordance with human nature and so is immediately related to what I refer to below as self-awareness. Any one model is, however, inadequate to a full understanding of the Christian mystery. From the perspective of sound educational practice and Christian experience, we may consider the development of morality from roughly three perspectives: behavioral, psychoanalytical, and developmental.

The Behavioral Perspective

B.F. Skinner, the doyen of behaviorism in America, affirms the total control of the individual by his culture and conditions and in this sense, parallels Calvin and his Puritan descendents. Raised in a fundamentalist Presbyterian home, Skinner came to admire the external control that many religions demonstrate, "for theologians have accepted the fact that man must be predetermined to do what an omniscient God knows he will do. . . ."[10] In Skinnerian terms, traditional Christianity has relied upon aversive controls, threats of punishment, to determine morality. God for Skinner (no doubt reflecting the tradition he came from) was the Judge rather than the Father. Skinner's work is filled with examples of religious controls; "He continually compares his proposed technology of behavior with the force that religion has for control."[11] In his *Beyond Freedom and Dignity*, he denies the existence of the autonomous man, that is, the man who possesses freedom, dignity, and discernment. For Skinner there is no internal dynamic, no struggle. There is, in fact, in behaviorism no "chosen evil." Behaviorism in the 20th century sees evil as "unchosen" and people as good or bad because their culture and condition-ing make them so.[12] There are only actions which society will judge as useful or not useful to itself.

I do not mention behavior just as one approach to moral education, but as an approach that upholds what I have been saying about the traditional approach to morality as action. Few religious educators in the patristic tradition will accept Skinner's extreme position that morality is purely behav-ioral, that man bears no responsibility for his actions or thoughts. But in spite of the evident distaste for Skinnerian techniques and philosophy among Christians, many of the techniques of the Church conform to his technology, from the gold stars in Sunday school to threats of losing your soul or gaining paradise. No Christian should be good because he wants to earn the kingdom of God;[13] although an ontological subtlety, the point is that he is good because he has already had the kingdom won for him by Christ.

The Church has traditionally dealt with morals and moral-ity either in terms of spiritual development (patristic) or in terms of controlling behavior (canonical).[14] Neither was adaequate since the former turned the Church into a cha-rismatic, antinomian fellowship and the latter turned it into a formal institution whose conditions for membership could be objectively determined and obliged. It had been believed that you produce ethical people by "telling" them how to behave, by moralizing, and by establishing regula-tions that set parameters within which they are permitted to behave for their own good and for the good of community.

The Church as institution, both before and after the *pax ecclesiae*, was superficially behavioristic; that is, it decreed behavior patterns appropriate to Christians, as for instance in the first part of the *Didache*, the *Catechetical Orations* of St Cyril of Jerusalem, and especially in the works of St John Chrysostom.[15] One of the problems faced by the Church, especially after the *pax ecclesiae*, was not in determining appropriate behavior, but in its inability as an institution to judge morality in terms of feeling and thinking—behavior that is not in the public domain. The problem of morality and behaviorism was evident to Gregory of Nazianzus, who wrote:

> (unlike that of the physician) is concerned with the hidden man of the heart, and our warfare is directed against that adversary and foe within us.[16]

As late as the late thirteenth century and early fourteenth century, Athanasius of Contantinople elaborated innumerable, tiresome rules, almost reflecting the burdensome regulations that guided Geneva under Calvin's Company of Pastors. What saved the Church from her canons, largely behavioral, were the saints and holy men, who displayed the integrated spiritual/moral life in their feelings, actions, and attitudes. There is an immediate integrating aspect to *askesis*, self-denial, which has hardly been explored as the basis for moral growth.[17] Yet even the hagiographical literature, which I would recommend as the basis for any treatment of moral life in the history of the Church, is unrealistic. A critical approach to this is in order as, for instance, when Gregory of Nazianzus writes that while Samuel may have been "holy" from his swaddling clothes, (I Sam 2:11), priests should not imagine, however, that they are automatically teachers of high estimation.[18] The changing of behavior, as an objective, is clearly inadequate. A person may indeed act morally and not be a Christian. Surely, the New Testament calls for a great deal more than simply conformity to the prescriptions of the Torah.

We can and must as Orthodox affirm that there are rules; there are rights and wrongs which are established by the Church and our own experience. Yet these rules say nothing about how the person is to feel. We must also affirm as

Christians that the Church is as interested in people's behavior as it is in the reason for their behavior. We must affirm with St Paul that the feelings and thinking behind the rules must have their sources in the people and not in the law; if all we have is the law, then we have condemnation (Romans 2:12; 3:20). Law does not and cannot transform; it can, however, provide the occasion for transformation. The law was and is a window for God's grace to act. Morality—thinking, feeling, acting—must come from within people and be a free response to that person's awareness of himself as a Christian believer. Rules are still the key; they are, however, parameters.

The early Church, assuming that the external reflected the internal, focused on rules as one way of determining external morality. The early Church, particularly in the catechumenate, set up proscribed professions for baptismal candidates, a period of time during which they could demonstrate their *worthiness*, and conditions under which it would not accept donations from contributors.[19] It is evident that the Church sought to legislate morality in a behavioristic sense. Yet the limitation was built into moral order; the Church admitted that all that could be controlled was that which fell into the *public domain*. The Church as institution shied away from any attempt to regulate conscience, intention, or attitudes, and, with the exceptions of hagiographical and spiritual treatises, we find no treatment of such. The fundamental elements of Christian morality sprang out of the search for the right relationship with God and with men; its fundamental principles were ascetical mutualism, and, since it happened in the community, can be understood conveniently as a socialization process.[20]

Behaviorism is inadequate to Church life and the growth of Christian moral attitude, behavior, and thinking. God is Our Father and not the Great Reinforcer. The fact that the

Church has been behavioristic is hard to dispute but should not provoke angry reactions. Behaviorism simply affirms that the Church could only legislate what it could measure as institution. Right behavior may, indeed, induce right feelings, as C.S. Lewis has affirmed, and as we have experienced;[21] it is, however, sadly inadequte, as the lives of the saints show. The psychosomatic unity of personhood permits this free interaction between being and doing; we become what we do and do what we become. It is radically limited as any approach affecting only one-third of the moral triangle I have posited. "We are to do what we are" is a truism that meets both the demands of self-awareness and the patristic notion of human freedom.[22] Behaviorism does not deal with discernment, *diakrisis*, which is an element focusing on the transformation of the mind and the heightening of the cognitive sense. Discernment is not solely cognitive but has a cognitive element, as Paul makes clear in Hebrews 5:14.

The Psychoanalytical Perspective

Opposed to Skinner and more in keeping with the patristic anthropology of the self-creating human person, sharing in God's work, are men such as Karl Rogers, Rollo May, and Abraham Maslow. Man is free and growth is from within, freely to be willed and freely to be shaped by guidance and discipline. The "teacher" as the guide is anathema to Skinner for whom teacher is "controller."

Ultimately, morality in a person, whether Christian or otherwise, depends on how he sees himself, how he sees his relationship to the world, and how he perceives his relationship to other people. Simply stated, from a psychoanalytical point of view a person will act in accordance with the manner in which he perceives himself. It is a mistake, therefore, to expect Christian behavior from an individual, let us say a teenager, unless he comes to be aware of himself as a Christian. It is equally mistaken to expect Godly behavior from a child who does not see himself as a God-centered person—a perception that cannot reasonably be expected to appear in a mature form before the age of thirteen. As a person perceives himself so he will tend to behave. From what does self-awareness derive? Self-awareness grows out of and is dependent upon how we treat children, what we tell them about themselves, who we tell them God is and what He says about them, and, finally, how they develop cognitively. The child, as we will see in the developmental portion, must be paced out of a quantitative, egocentric, microscopic vision of himself and his morality as one of do's and don'ts, pleasing and not pleasing others, punishments and rewards, to a macroscopic vision of himself in endless process of growth and union with God, out of which springs ethical behavior. To enable his growth, we can effectively use the tools made available by Lawrence Kohlberg's cognitive-developmental model to be discussed later.[23]

We can also turn to the New Testament with its psycho-analytic emphasis on the use and process of modeling, which is in the affective domain as opposed to the cognitive and behavioral. In the psychoanalytical understanding, the child seeks to win the approval of his parents or a significant adult by identifying with that adult's pattern of behavior. That is, a model is that person whom a child trusts and loves and as a result copies in a dynamic manner. This, of course, applies immediately to the Christian family, but also speaks indirectly to the emphasis placed on Christ as the model, par excellence, for all Christians. In the New Testament not only is the teaching of Christ foundational for morality but also the very person of the Incarnate Logos, both as model and as enabler.

The fact remains, however, that the command to love

one's neighbor does not tell us what, when, and how to do this. Rudolph Bultmann held that Christians would know how to do this intuitively, if they stood in the power of love.[24] This is not very helpful! For Origen, Christ is the model of the ethical life who at the same time makes that ethical life possible.[25] Modeling and natural law are the extent of Origen's moral formation. St Basil, however, takes up the same Scriptural theme:

> For in them [Scriptures] are not only found the precepts of conduct, but also the lives of saintly men, recorded and handed down to us, lie before us like living images of God's government, for our imitation of their good work.[26]

In his summary of his moral teaching, *Ta ethika*, Basil, who also considers at length the model value of the Old Testament saints,[27] insists on Christ as the pattern to whom Christians must conform.[28] Gregory of Nazianzus, a master of pastoral responsibility, highlighted this modeling approach to moral formation in his *Oration on the Occasion of the Funeral of Basil the Great*. He notes that Basil had "at home a model of virtue in well-doing" and he traveled with this model, his father, "without being left far behind in his lofty impulses toward virtue. . . drawing outlines of perfection before the time of perfection arrived."[29]

The Developmental Perspective
New Testament

The quality of discernment depends on the person's mental development and the actualization of that development through experience, especially relationships and teaching. The New Testament gives specific information on the place of the mind and mental discernment: the rational aspect of moral life is added to the affective as expressed in modeling. Paul, for instance, refers to the Gentiles as "darkened in their understanding, alienated from the life of God because of the ignorance that is in them" (Ephesians 4:17ff); again, the Gentiles are suffering from "senseless minds" (Romans 1:21) and the Jews are afflicted with "hardened minds" (I Corinthians 3:14). For Paul, the renewal of the mind, the *nous*, is the basic renewal, initiating the ongoing metamorphosis of being changed into the likeness of God. For instance, Paul urges the Romans to "think with sober judgement" in order to use their gifts responsibly (Romans 12:3). Forell notes in his analysis of ethical patterns in the New Testament and specifically in Galatians (5:14) that

> it is the mind and the application of reason which enable Christians to articulate the meaning of this summary of the law in the concrete situations in which they find themselves.[30]

Christian ethics is not *sui generis*, based on direct inspiration that guides the Church and the person at every instant. It is a multifaceted phenemenon, rooted in a renewed mind, which enables the Christian to live for God and his neighbor. It is, much as Paul explains in Timothy, an *epignosis aletheias* (II Timothy 2:24-25). Origen picks up the same theme and notes that it is reason and not custom that enables people to distinguish between wise and foolish laws and make intelligent ethical decisions. Morality for Christians clearly has a cognitive as well as an affective aspect.

Patristic Tradition

No one is born moral or religious; regardless of what the "image" of God in man means, we know that it is fulfilled within us over a period of time and with development. Just as morality cannot be coerced behavioristically, neither does it occur automatically. Gregory of Nazianzus, a much underestimated contributor to our understanding of human nature, noted that the teacher/bishop was to draw people to Christ by his own virtue and not by the force of authority. For what is involuntary, apart from its being the result of oppression, is neither meritorious nor durable. "For what is forced. . . when set free, returns to what it was before, but that which is a result of choice is both most legitimate and enduring, for it is preserved by the bond of good will."[31]

What we have in the patristic tradition is dynamic anthropology and personhood as the focus of history and salvation; personality development is foundational to Christian theology and I think it is in the context of personhood that Orthodox pedagogues can make a genuine contribution to contemporary pedagogical issues. It is in the developing person, the human person *in via, en prokopio* (Luke 2:52), that we can as pastors and parents make contact with contemporary developmental psychology. It seems to me that the starting point is the *image* and *likeness* distinction made first by St Clement of Alexandria, the first ethical theologian of the Church, and then developed by other Fathers— particularly St Basil,[32] to whom we can trace the dynamic approach to human life and interior existence. This distinction has served to express the patristic belief that man is *in via* or *en prokopio*; not complete as born into a fallen world, he is nonetheless endowed with the necessary tools to become so as he pursues a life with God.[33] St Irenaeus of Lyons, claims that man was created a "child," emerging from a state of innocence and destined to grow to a state of maturity.

The Fathers defined the "image" as man's rational faculties.[34] The human mind, reason, properly used was a route to God.[35] Man contained the capacity for moral perfection in potential and it was required of him to develop from the stage of childhood holiness to approximate the holiness of God in accord with the command of Matthew 5:48.[36] Grace is necessary and love is foundational, but man is an active sharer in his own moral perfection if through no other means than a willingness to receive the grace to be healed. The patristic views of man as being created in order to share in God's life, in order to be active in accordance with his own destiny, as determined by God, excludes the purely passive role of man in his own salvation, as in the Augustinian tradition of Luther, Calvin, and Skinner.[37]

Self-awareness is keyed to the patristic notion of man as the "image" of God. Looking within can lead to the discovery of the Creator and the enhancement of the self. The ideal of moral/spiritual development focusing on awareness abounds in the Fathers; and I would add that it is only out of this cultivation of self-awareness that the moral life of the Christian can develop. (Romans 7:15-25; Matthew 26:38-43; Mark 14:34-40; 13:33-37; Luke 21:24-36; Ephesians 5:14-15). Clement of Alexandria in Book III of *The Instructor* affirms that "the greatest of all lessons [is] to know oneself. For only if one knows himself, he will know God and knowing God, he will be made like God. . . ."[38] As I have said, it was for the first 500 years the peculiar Orthodox approach to focus on personhood as the locus of theological thought, but specifically the personhood of Christ which in the Chalcedonian definition is the analogue of human personhood. Personhood is based on awareness and self understanding and no one is born with it fully developed. Personhood, image of God, and moral development are intimately tied together.

Gregory of Nazianzus sardonically refers to Samuel's being *holy* from swaddling clothes as no excuse for anyone to believe that he can be a pastor and teacher without working at it through study and preparation.[39] Gregory observed later in the same work:

The wiser of the Hebrews tell us that there was of

old among the Hebrews a most excellent and praiseworthy law, that every age was not entrusted with the whole of the Scripture, inasmuch as this would not be the more profitable course, since the whole of it is not at once intelligible to everyone, and its more recondite parts would by their apparent meaning, do a very great injury to most people. Some portions, therefore, whose exterior [apparent meaning] is unexceptional, are from the first permitted and common to all; while others are only entrusted to those who have attained their twenty-fifth year, viz., such as hide their mystical beauty under a mean-looking cloak, to be the reward of diligence and an illustrious life; flashing forth and presenting itself only to those whose mind has been purified on the ground that this age alone can be superior to the body, and properly rise from the letter to the spirit.[40]

If something is presented to those who are immature, in the "habit of babes," and beyond their strength, they will probably be "overwhelmed and oppressed, owing to the inability of their mind. . . to digest and appropriate what is offered to it."[41] If you try to overfeed them or misfeed them, Gregory notes, they will not be strengthened but annoyed:

. . . and with good reason, for they will not be strengthened according to Christ, nor make that laudable increase, which the word produces in one who is rightly fed, by making him a perfect man, and bringing him to the measure of spiritual stature. (Ephesians 4:13)[42]

What we see in the Fathers is patristic vision of an "active person," in process of developing as opposed to a passive, receptive person, as product. Human, personal actions are *real* and make a difference.

The two negative factors we have experienced educationally in the development of full Christian personhood were (1) the absolutization of adulthood as the pattern for childhood and the corresponding perception of the child as a miniature adult and (2) morality as a divinely given series of rules and regulations to be obeyed out of fear. Neither of these corresponds to a patristic anthropology,[43] in which moral reasoning, as the ability to reason generally, develops slowly and in stages.

The centrality of self-awareness to moral development is seen to have a cognitive element, and we must never miss the fact that the spiritual essence of moral development, repentance, in fact, included a cognitive "turning around," a *metanoia*, a transforming of the mind. Second, patristic anthropology assumed an active agent. Man is what he does and does what he is; man's choices and actions were valuable for salvation or damnation. Unlike behaviorism, human activities made a difference; the concept of synergy is used to summarize this active anthropology. Third, we see in the Fathers a process at odds with a behaviorist product/performance approach to growth into the life of God.

The patristic anthropology did not speak about moral behavior as such; it did not speak about right or wrong but about growing into the "image and likeness" of God. Patristic morality was not behavior; it was being (ontology), having as its ultimate goal the assimilation of the person to God, participation and union with God, through the humanity of Christ.

Self-Awareness

Developmentalism tells us what we can reasonably expect in terms of developing personhood and self-awareness as a basis for Christian education and moral development. In this sense developmentalism is descriptive and not prescriptive. We can get an idea of the normal stage of self-awareness of children at different ages, and it is in this context that we are able to speak of sin. If a person possesses a certain awareness of himself and acts out of keeping with that awareness then we can speak of personal sin as an internal contradiction, a destruction of the person's very humanity, which humanity is to be his window, his contact with the incarnate God. We can therefore speak of sin as self-destruction. But we cannot speak of sin unless a person has a healthy self-awareness. When a five-year-old refuses to share a toy, we cannot speak of sin, because his self-awareness is heavily egocentric and hence that toy is still perceived as part of him; sharing it may in fact appear to his mind as a type of death.[44] What is clear is that children have developmental tasks at certain stages; for instance, when the two-year-old continually refuses to do what the parents want, it may either be looked at as an act of outrageous defiance or as an ethical necessity representing his need to affirm his distinctness. He is acting, in fact, out of self-awareness, albeit a limited one. The same thrust for independence tends to be repeated among adolescents.[45]

Similarly, we cannot expect self-denial in the ascetical sense until a person has developed a sense of self-as-separate; neither can we expect sharing freely of goods unless the child has first reached the age where he has the notion of possession. There are numerous other examples of how the developmental approach to morality can clarify many problems for church educators. Keep in mind that as Christians we seek healthy emotional and spiritual personalities, and the two-year-old, affirming his distinctness, is acting out of a normal sense of self-awareness and we should expect nothing else. Knowing this, we have no right to destroy the child's functioning as long as it does not threaten the parents and family.

Adolescence is another and perhaps even a classic example of morality springing out of age-related self-awareness. As anyone who has worked or lived with adolescents understands, they are in a period of transition whose leading characteristics have been well described by Piaget[46] and Erikson.[47] The years from approximately 11 to 20 are characterized by such rapid changes that the only consistency in behavior is inconsistency. Hence, the teen's self-awareness often vacillates between that of the child and that of the adult. Trying to act as a whole person, he produces an apparent series of confusing moral behavior; wholeness for the adolescent is necessarily relative.

Considering this in light of what was said earlier on behaviorism, we see that just as a given state of self-awareness gives rise to a particular set of actions, so certain actions can heighten a particular self-awareness. A clear contact is possible here between a psychoanalytic and a cognitive-developmental approach. The two-year-old becomes more aware of himself as distinct by acting on his own. This is sound patristic anthropology and, in fact, represents a justification for a type of behaviorism. "So not only does a man do what he is according to his self-awareness, he becomes what he does."[48]

What we can conclude then from a consideration of self-awareness is that given the gradual development of the human person and his self-awareness, the moral content of a person's actions will be relative. When a mature adult imitates the actions of a two-year-old's egocentric disruption, we can then speak of sin or immorality. We cannot demand or expect from a growing child or adolescent the same kind of actions and behavior we have a right to expect from a mature person. It is after the Hebrews became aware of the covenant with Yahweh the commandments then made sense, and to violate them was to violate who the Hebrews were as a convenanted people.

In essence, therefore, an immoral act is one that is untrue to a healthy self-concept, one which by definition contradicts the very being of the person. Perhaps our freedom rests in our ability to contradict our very being and destroy ourselves. The result of persistent immoral acts, therefore, is to produce a distorted self-awareness and a perverse and perverted personality.

There remains a norm beyond a developmental or psychoanalytical self-awareness, and that is the nature of humanity as a creature of God. Ultimately, in patristic anthropology, the moral norm is within the person himself—both in his given nature, bent by sin, yet in the image of the Creator, and in his consciousness of what is moral. This means that a Christian must not only understand what it means to be moral, but must also have an understanding of what God reveals as good and bad through the revelation of Jesus Christ as the ideal man, the man who is with God, and finally who is God. This is the foundational morality of the Gospel; not the do's and don'ts, not Matthew 21, but the *very person of* Jesus Christ. All the rules and regulations can make sense only after the person becomes aware of himself as a brother/sister of Christ. Moral training is not then accidental; it happens by how we relate to the child, what we tell the child about who he is, and how he develops. I believe that developmental research helps to set the parameter to do this most effectively. For educators, the centrality of self-awareness to moral development highlights the educational process as a serious enterprise.

The Developmental Model

We must now turn to the revolution in psychology brought about by the so-called developmental psychologists—Eric Erikson,[49] Jean Piaget,[50] and Lawrence Kohlberg.[51] Erikson's sympathetic approach to religious categories and his application of his stage/crisis approach to human emotional maturation bears directly on elements of morality. For Erikson, there are periods in people's lives during which foundational elements for Christian morality, liturgics, and faith develop. These have been largely ignored by Orthodox, but were developed in an earlier chapter of this work.[52] Consider, for example, the importance of trust, autonomy, initiative, and industry to moral development.[53] Especially consider these in relation to the work of Gordon Allport in the 1950's in the *Nature of Prejudice* and the dysfunction caused by the inability to trust.[54]

Jean Piaget's work, upon which Kohlberg based his own research, is a significant place to begin this discussion of cognitive developmental aspects of moral thinking. As with any aspect of an educational enterprise, it is essential to understand its theoretical presuppositions as well as its educational strategies. This effort will enable us to evaluate Kohlberg's theory for positive application to a Church school or home setting without blinding ourselves to its larger philosophical or spiritual implications, both positive and negative.

Many teachers and pastors are already familiar with Piaget's stages of cognitive development. For our purposes, Piaget posits, however, a two-stage theory of moral development—heteronomous and autonomous. He investigates the child's concept of justice and his attitude toward the violation of mores.[55] Kohlberg also accepted from Piaget his epistemological principle that (1) there are stages of moral growth which parallel the stages of cognitive growth, (2) the person is active in the knowing process, (3) each stage is a structural whole, and (4) each stage is *appropriate* to the age of the person.[56] His sensori-motor stage describes a purely self-satisfying morality, a "sphincter-control morality"; good or bad, in this case of toilet performance, is determined by the reward or punishment which the behavior occasions. There is no morality strictly speaking. Good and bad, right and wrong, are determined elsewhere than in the individual; his relationships with others are characterized by an essential inequality. This is the childhood level of the respect for authority and power; because the adults surrounding the child are bigger and in control of the environment, the child is *obliged* to obey. It is a one-way relationship productive of a morality of constraint. The adult and the child are playing the game with a different set of rules and by the very nature of the adult-child relationship and the size and control exercised by the adult, there can be no equality and consequently no genuine morality. From a Christian perspective, we cannot here speak of morality but only the imposition of a behavior pattern that is pleasing to the adult and which exists for the adult's sake. It is this heteronomous stage which is necessary in laying the foundation for the control of emotions and the control the individual will later exercise in meeting his needs.

A child is never mutual with his parents, regardless of how democratic parents try to be in the home.[57] *Power* characterizes the relations, whether we as adults are aware of it or not. Elements of democracy can and must be introduced into the home, but democracy as a concept and a practice can be seriously misplaced in a home setting and with young children.[58] And since moral development is not simply maturation of innate potential but derives also from interaction, this heteronomous period becomes particularly important for the foundation of conscience and the learning of rules. The maturation of mental structures makes moral development possible but not automatic. An eight-year-old may well be more ethical than a 35-year-old criminal, for instance.[59] Bruno Bettelheim notes that Piaget's work is or may be conditioned by his location in Geneva, with its middle-class culture and relatively stable society, and that in America heteronomy may be abbreviated since peers play a larger role earlier in life. "The parents become less and less domineering in the child's life, the relations betwen the parent and the child less unilateral. . . ." He notes, by way of support, the American child's earlier entrance into nursery school.[60] The possible significance of this in Piaget's terms is that children can learn the morality of cooperation *earlier*, but this says nothing about bypassing the heteronomous stage completely. I am not sure how significant this factor is, given the sheer physical size of the parents and adults around the children and their limited contact with other children, even in schools. As the child matures, possibly in the early teens, he is able to move into autonomous aspects of moral development, characterized by mutuality, cooperation, and regard for others, refined by the give-and-take of peer interaction.

The possibility for this mutuality begins, however, around the age of seven and progresses until late teenage years by which time it should be an internal morality, freely chosen and freely maintained. Autonomy does not describe or prescribe moral actions or moral values; it merely describes the ability of a person to act independently of force, coercion, and pressure in determining his behavior and value system. For Piaget, autonomous morality is rooted in cooperation and mutuality; a sense and experience of community is abolutely fundamental to its development.[61] For Piaget mature morality is social morality rooted in social interaction. The moral goal of mutuality is foundational to an Orthodox conception of social and monastic life and immediately related to monastic *askesis*. For us Christians it has been a self-evident reality that the saints are essentially social.[62] One need only mention St Basil's Lesser Rules and their focus on mutuality.

Lawrence Kohlberg of Harvard University took the cognitive developmental work of Piaget and constructed a model of moral development which is essentially cognitive. That is, Kohlberg focuses not on specific actions or beliefs but rather on the structure of moral thinking—the manner in which people reason through a *dilemma* or resolve a cognitive *dissonance* or discomfort. Hence, the key to Kohlberg is to see this as a cognitive model that describes patterns of reasoning in ethical situations, aiming at ethical adequacy in the application of generalized principles, such as justice. His schema and the techniques it uses do not seek to impose values, but to trace and encourage ethical thinking and valuing processes. It is of note to educators and pastors, because his schema employs a technique that may be used to heighten cognitive sensitivity to moral issues.

While Piaget assumes two basic moral stages, Kohlberg assumes from his research three levels of two stages each for a total of six definable stages. Kohlberg is valuable because his stages are convenient and because he presupposes elements, albeit not religious, that are congenial to the patristic pattern I have established for process, active agency, and personal responsibility. As I consider Kohlberg, I shall try to integrate Piaget's cognitive and Erikson's emotional findings into an integrated presentation of an effective system for the pastor, the parent, and the teacher.

From Piaget, Kohlberg accepts the following fundamental epistemological principles: 1) there are stages to human development; 2) the stages are marked by qualitative as well as quantitative distinctions; 3) the stages are sequential, hierarchical, and invariant; 4) each stage has a structural schema to handle moral issues so that a person's responses to a moral issue are not right or wrong, but rather adequate or inadequate to the stage; 5) ethics is defined in terms of the way we judge or the form which thinking takes in reaching a conclusion, so that moral content is distinguished from moral judgment and morality is limited to cognitive judgment;[63] 6) people tend to prefer higher order thinking to that done at lower stages, even when the higher stage is above their predominant stage; and finally, 7) development is a movement toward greater epistemological and ethical maturity in applying the principle of justice. Cognitive awareness, however, is not a given; it develops in the context of mental development and environmental interaction—family, Church, and society. This last point is significant for Christian educators because even the given of Piagetian mental development is conditioned by the social element over which the Church and the family have some input, as in the development of the person's self-awareness. Even the ten commandments can make sense only if the believer is *aware* of his relationship with God as a covenant. In an Orthodox context this happens in the Church as a community, as has been made clear in an earlier chapter.[64]

Kohlberg's work began in 1958, when, through a longitudinal study of 75 American boys, he created a schema paralleling that of Piaget. He later continued this on a cross-cultural basis tracing the development of the concept of justice, the highest moral virtue for him, in people in a variety of cultural settings.[65] Kohlberg's findings are descriptive and are in no way meant to be prescriptive. In fact, it is when they are applied prescriptively that they become dangerous as guidelines.[66] The value of stage-development theory and its application to moral development is that it enables pastors, parents, and educators better to understand what is happening to the people and enables them to establish reasonable expectations. Although this is basically a statistical approach, Kohlberg, Piaget, and Erikson claim that its implications and conclusions are not limited by statistical samples. Knowing how people are probably reasoning and which particular factors are primary at a particular age helps us to be more realistic in our expectations, our teaching, and our dealing with their behavior. It helps us as adults to see what it is to be adult and what it is to be child; it helps us to avoid applying the virtues of one to the other and to be able to detect which characteristics are normal and which are abnormal. In fact, it enables educators to break out of the Freudian application of the adult model to the child.[67] The limits of moral thinking, like the limits of cognition in general, can be taken as opportunities. We must take them as indicators of what we can do and what we can expect, much as Gregory Nazianzus, from the people with whom we are working at certain ages.

The schema describes the formation of conscience as a developmental process in which people move from one stage to another, and, by definition, to higher and more adequate stages of reasoning until they can reason in terms of the highest universal principle which Kohlberg identifies with justice. It is an age-associated, but not limited process, inasmuch as it (1) assumes the existence of certain mental structures and (2) presupposes meaningful experience. It is not, however, necessary with age, and grown criminals may have a less developed sense of right and wrong than a ten-year-old. Potential virtues need cultivation and nurturing, which come only with time, experience, and concrete instruction and models.

Kohlberg's work is the theoretical framework for moral development most frequently discussed by theologians and public school administrators. It is also the theory that is most frequently attacked by conservatives and fundamentalists as well as by some thoughtful educators. Where some Christians feel uncomfortable with Kohlberg is in his conclusion that the form of moral judgment is distinguishable from the content of moral decision, and is actually more important. Morality is the way we think about the application of rules when faced with a dilemma, and it is defined in terms of the formal character of moral judgment, not in terms of content or behavior.[68] He does not ask what morality is, but how a person becomes moral.[69] The Orthodox parent or educator must never lose sight of the fact that moral thinking and reasoning skills are tools, sharpening the powers of discernment (*diakrisis*). Kohlberg has himself affirmed in a lecture to the Religious Education Association, knowledge (of right and wrong) is necessary but not sufficient to moral judgement, and judgement is necessary but not sufficient to moral action.

Religious educators have, however, been drawn to it because it emphasizes certain fundamental Christian principles which, in spite of its weakness, are important—freedom, responsibility, *diakrisis*, conscience. I am drawn to it because it seems congenial to elements of patristic anthropology—process, personhood, self-knowledge, and the natural differences among people.[70] It is a theory which in addition to this seems counter to the Puritan/Calvinist tendency inherent in the American child-rearing and child-education practices that reduce the child to a miniature adult and try to educate him *out* of his "childness." In addition, it carries with it no moral values except those of the centrality of justice, which do not affect the research findings. Finally, it advances a tested technique for the enhancement of the person's moral thinking ability. Of all theories of moral development, Kohlberg's takes least account of the home and minimizes the environment; when he does work with environment he emphasizes the school more than the home. Nevertheless, the techniques that characterize his research can be used in the home.

Kohlbergian Dilemmas

In Kohlberg's research, people of various ages and from different backgrounds were presented with problematic situations, dilemmas, which were designed to place the person in a state of tension or "cognitive dissonance." It is interesting to note here that this procedure is not unique to Kohlberg, but was actually used by the ancient Greeks and the Christian Fathers. St Ambrose, for instance, makes use of the classic life-boat situation from Cicero. He notes:

> Suppose there were two to be rescued from a sinking ship—both of them wise men—and only one small plank, should both seize it to save themselves? or should one give place to the other?

Cicero answered:

> Why, of course, one should give place to the other, but the other must be one whose life is more valuable either for its own sake or for that of his country.[71]

Ambrose, however, jumped past Cicero's reasoning to one of Kohlberg's highest stages, rejected utilitarian categories completely, and affirmed that ethical questions must be referred to a universal principle:

> Some ask whether a wise man ought in case of a shipwreck to take a away a plank from a ignorant sailor? Although it seems better for the common good that a wise man rather than a fool should escape from shipwreck, yet I do not think that a Christian, a just and wise man, ought to save his own life by the death of another.[72]

Self-denial and the service of a brother/sister is the universal principle which makes the philosopher's arguments meaningless.

Perhaps Kohlberg's most famous case is the so-called Heinz dilemma:[73]

> In Europe a woman was near death from a special kind of cancer. There was one drug that the doctors thought might save her. It was a form of radium that a druggist in the same town had

recently discovered. The drug was expensive to make, but the druggist was charging ten times what the drug cost to make. He paid $200 for the radium and charged $2000 for a small dose of the drug. The sick woman's husband, Heinz, went to everyone he knew to borrow the money, but he could only get together about $1000 which is half of what it cost. He told the druggist that his wife was dying, and ask him to sell it cheaper or let him pay later. But the druggist said, "No, I discovered the drug and I'm going to make money from it." Should Heinz steal the drug?

This story represents a dilemma by which Kohlberg forced people of different ages and moral stages to take a stand and reach a solution. What concerned Kohlberg, however, was not the conclusion the person reached but the process by which he reached it. He discovered that though people differed in their conclusions, the reasoning processes by which they arrived at their conclusions showed patterns of similarity which he could categorize according to one of three levels of two stages each, and roughly corresponding to Piaget's age distribution for cognitive development.

Kohlberg's six stages correspond to three levels which he defines in terms of the child's relations to *community*—(1) pre-conventional, (2) conventional, and (3) post-conventional. As we consider each of the three levels and their 6 stages, I will highlight their key elements and relate them to Erikson's (emotional) crises and Piaget's (cognitive) stages. I will also apply them to the peculiar needs of Christian development, especially by focusing on the role of the concept of *person* in relationship to the theme of *community*. It is of note here that Kohlberg's three levels focus both positively and negatively on the role of community, a category central to Orthodox theological and psychological development.[74]

Kohlberg's Schema

Level I: Pre-Conventional. At this level the child is oc-
cupied with himself. This corresponds roughly to Piaget's
description of the child from birth to 7 years (sensori-motor
and pre-operational stages);[75] he is highly egocentric and
this appears to be one of the reasons why Kohlberg refers to
this level as pre-conventional in the sense of being pre-
communal. It also corresponds to Piaget's heteronomous
stage of moral development; Kohlberg describes it as a
period when the child is preoccupied with power and
authority. The child, developing in a non-mutual setting, is
controlled by physical power—"daddy and mommy are
bigger" is the basis of discipline and so we cannot speak of
morality in any formal sense of the term. It is a period of
unilateral relationships, with adults getting their way by
force. Parents by virtue of their size and control of money,
for instance, are in fact coercive. Quantitative effects are the
key to understanding his behavior and his morality. All rules
are from above, God, or parents, and are seen in terms of
physical and hedonistic consequences.

Stage 1: Punishment and Obedience. At this stage an
action is thought to be good or bad depending on the
physical consequences of the act. Morality is therefore largely quantitative, or scalar, having no direction or absolute
value. Hence, for a child of this stage, breaking five tea cups
on purpose is not as bad as breaking ten by accident. The
child does what Piaget refers to as *centering*; the child is
perception-bound and focuses on one (usually the most
prominent) aspect of the physical incident; in this case the
number of cups.[76] The situation is judged by its consequences and not by the intentions of the actors. They have a
limited notion of someone else's feelings.[77] Similarly, killing
the president is worse than killing the local butcher,
because the president is more important. The stage 1 person

does not use such phrases as "he didn't mean to do this or that," because he hasn't yet developed the ability to see something from someone else's emotional or physical perspective. Hence, qualities such as sharing and reciprocity really make no sense at this stage and are quite dependent on achieving notions of possession and a sense of other people's feelings. In response to the Heinz dilemma, a stage one child *might* respond: "Heinz shouldn't steal the drug because he might get caught and go to jail."

Stage 2: Instrumental Relativist Orientation. At this stage, the child is still pre-conventional, heteronomous,[78] and takes consideration chiefly for himself, although no longer controlled solely by physical consequence. His perspective is still controlled by his egocentrism and is perception-bound. Toward the end of this stage the child will begin to try to break out of himself and his limited perception as he begins to grow into a sense of community. The two movements are spiritually inseparable.

A right action is that which satisfies one's own needs and only occasionally perhaps the needs of others; sharing is still not an easy practice and the notion that "it is better to give than to receive" makes little sense. If notions of sharing, mutuality, and fairness do exist, they exist in self-serving categories: "You scratch my back and I'll scratch yours." God is largely a power figure to be feared; a figure who will punish, reward, or make deals depending on the child's needs. The child is still confined to a heteronomous situation and ruled by a non-mutual relationship with adults around him. He will start to break out of this between the ages of seven and thirteen as he attempts to understand motives and his own personhood and that of others. A Stage 2 response to the Heinz Dilemma might be: "Heinz should steal the drug because he needs his wife."

Level 2: Conventional. The first major mental/moral revolution in the life of the human person seems to occur sometime around the age of 7 years, the proverbial "age of reason," when we expect, not without some justification, that the child will be able to judge right from wrong and will be able to share in the sacrament of confession. This level is referred to as Conventional because the maturing person conforms to and confirms accepted standards and usage.

Perhaps the most significant aspect of Kohlberg's work, for Christian educators, is at this level because it focuses on the normative role of the community.[79] From this description it is relatively clear that the two stages of moral growth in Level 2 focus on the community and the family, the subjects of the preceding two chapters of this book. However, which community, nation, church, neighborhood the child tries to emulate depends on the values of the child's family, since conformity and loyalty characterize this level.

At the second level we also begin the first major revolution in moral thinking; it is the period which describes for Erikson the emotional explosion of *initiative* (vs. guilt) and *industry* (vs. inferiority), the characteristics that tie the child creatively and cooperatively to a community in a productive interaction. It is the period when, in Piaget's terms, the child exhibits what is referred to as *role projection, role taking*, and *moral imagination*. This makes cooperative and communal life possible and at the same time forms the basis for Christian morality—love, mutuality, and *diakrisis*. There can be no morality in the sense of mutualistic ethics unless the person can project himself into someone else's position; and for the sake of integrated development, the child also develops the ability to perceive *physically* elements in his environment from a perspective other than his own. James Fowler's foundational work in faith development has indicated that "perspective taking" is also one of the seven aspects of faith development. Perspective taking begins with egocentrism and moves toward a fully mutual world view.[80] The ethical foundations are clearly tied to the cognitive and the social. Selma Fraiberg, a psychologist at the University of Michigan, writes of the modern "disease of non-attachment" that it is distinguished by

> incapacity of the person to form human bonds. . . . In the absence of human ties a conscience cannot be formed, even the qualities of self-observation and self-criticism fail to develop.[81]

This is exactly what St Basil intuited when he wrote that when we live alone, we can wash no one's feet. Non-social individuals are handicapped in social, spiritual, and moral activity and were the subject of my consideration in an earlier chapter, when I discussed the dysfunction of "privatism."[82]

Children at this period are also consolidating their move from so-called parallel play to cooperative or social play. Formerly children played next to one another, but did not play together. They were, in effect, playing two separate games with two separate sets of rules. Now they can and do play *together*. *Play* itself now becomes fundamental to the further development of the mental structures that permit or accommodate social and moral development. Play, in this sense, must be taken quite seriously as a developmental mode affecting everything from the social to the liturgical growth of the child. Play, Puritan dread notwithstanding,[83] is part of the creative process of moral and spiritual development. Erikson notes that at around the age of seven the child demonstrates the inclination toward play, fantasy, and games. Games "with their interplay of free will and determined rules and laws lay the foundation for the child's moral education."[84] So then the child develops the ability to project, to imagine, to work and play with others his own age, to be aware of a community outside of the family and the demands of that community. The child begins to speak in terms of intentions and motives, his own and others. At this point he is ready for meaningful participation in the sacrament of confession.

It is at this age and during this level that a child's sense of freedom must be encouraged, what Erikson calls his initiative identity. His being placed in communal situations is foundational to this further development and should be a primary focus of parents and church schools during this period. The child is ready for social interaction and will characteristically try to determine how he fits in with communities, including the parish when the Church is central to the parents' values. It is common for a child to say, seeing his father talking to a stranger, "Who is he? Who is he to me?" Social interaction is one way children have of clarifying their thinking and learning that *their* (egocentric) view is not the only way of perceiving something.

Play as well as intergenerational activities must be part of the parish's educational ministry. In addition, the liturgy is particularly important; many psychologists relate the child's play to pre-liturgical development, which we as pastors and church educators cannot afford to ignore. It is, as we shall see, a period that calls for allowing the child to work, build, and share in the work of the parish as an expression of his industry. To learn the respective roles and rules of the liturgy should be keyed to this period of life.

Although Kohlberg's educational application is primarily in the school context, I would like to note here that parents can encourage moral development at this conventional level by the use of similar responsibility-sharing activities and especially value discussions in the home. Discussion is central at this period because it enables the child to use the new reasoning powers he is attaining, such as freedom from his perception, his ability to perceive intention, and his ability to project. This is especially true of the discussion of the Christian implication of current events, say, at the dinner table. Kohlberg himself notes:

> With regard to the family, the disposition of parents to allow or encourage dialogue on values issues is one of the clearest determinants of moral stage advance in children. Such an exchange of viewpoints and attitudes is part of what we term "role taking opportunities."[85]

It must be pointed out that such an effort on the part of Christian parents implies a risk: there is no guarantee that children will agree with the position of the parents. John Elias of Fordham University, however, points out the need for specifically Christian input to Kohlberg's approach:

> Parents who want to include the religious dimension in moral development must, however, supplement Kohlberg's ideas on the primacy of justice and moral reasoning (skills) with specifically religious motivation and concerns.[86]

In an otherwise secular system, Kohlberg offers Christian parents and parishes *windows* for action and for bringing in "bottom lines" (rules), if for no other reason than to establish a frame of reference, a basis for judgement.

The Conventional Level is the movement outward, away from egocentrism, toward a greater sensitivity to rules, the community, and the needs and motives of others. Evil, to infer from Selma Fraiberg's quote above, is isolation and self-centeredness. Obeying God, his rules, and the rules of the Church provides the occasion for genuine community and connectedness. The Church, the church school, and the youth group must provide this connection. This emphasis on social awareness, group values, cooperation, projection, moral imagination, and rules is evident in Kohlberg's application of the two stages of level two.

Stage 3: Good Boy and Nice Girl Orientation. At this stage morality for the child is whatever pleases others and especially significant, trusted others in the child's social interaction. Depending on the values of the family, this "significant other" may be a parish priest, a church school teacher, a school teacher, scout leader, etc. The child seeks their approval and in seeking their approval demonstrates a need to conform to and play the expected role, usually by the majority, or what the majority considers "natural" behavior. Here the role-modeling behavior discussed earlier in this chapter is important because the hero, the model, represents the values of the community; in this context the saint, the parish priest, or the father in the family represents the values of the community, in this case the Church. It should be evident at this point that the values of the parents, family, and community in which the child finds his security are the values he will emulate and by which he will find models in the "world" outside of the family. "Turn the other cheek," for example, is nonsense because it serves no social function unless the child comes from a community that values such self-effacement in the public domain.

For the first time, as already noted, the child can speak in terms of "intentions" of the actor—"He didn't mean that" or "He means well" is commonly heard. A stage three response to the Heinz dilemma might be: "Stealing is really bad, but Heinz doesn't mean [intend] to be a thief. He is doing something out of love for his wife." Or "It's only natural for a husband to steal for his wife in a case like this." Or "What would people say if he did not steal?" Or "Stealing is bad because it displeases God."

Stage 4: Law and Order. This stage represents a relatively rigid commitment to the authority of an abstract; the law, for instance, established by the community must be obeyed, whether good or bad. Loyalty to a law-making body is a virtue. Something is done, not for approval, but for conformity, which is primary. We are no longer in the realm of children, and Kohlberg has estimated that one-third of American adults fall into this stage of development. Right behavior consists in doing one's duty, showing respect for authority, and maintaining the social order for its own sake. God at this cognitive level is the great and good lawgiver. The law possesses an almost sacred character; the same would apply to those who affirm without reason a rigorous application of the canons in all situations, with no critical questioning. There can be no such thing as civil obedience, because the law is concrete, *sui generis*, and not a reflection of some higher principle. The response to the Heinz dilemma might be: "Heinz should not steal the drug because it is against the law. Even when tempted to steal, we are obliged to keep the law. However, he might steal the drug out of duty to his wife." The operative words here are "obliged" and "duty." "If everyone stole we would have chaos" marks the social (i.e., conventional) emphasis of this level of reasoning.

Level 3: Post-Conventional. The third level, as the name implies, goes beyond the community norm, what is agreed upon as acceptable; it falls into the realm of higher and/or personal values. The person is no longer conditioned by a need to be rewarded or to belong, or by approval of authority, or by the law as absolute. Law is relative and is designed to serve the good of all. Post-conventional reasoning moves beyond the need to serve self or the community. Morality becomes, in Piaget's terms, an autonomous morality; the person, based on his set of values and sense of good, functions "on his own."

We probably cannot speak about autonomous morality until a person is around the age of twelve, although many people never reach this level. Moral values reside in conformity to standards which exist apart from the endorse-

ment of any group (or community), personal need, or identification with a group. There can be no "My country, right
or wrong. . ." approach. No "Whatever the institutional
Church says. . . ." It is a morality of ultimate value and
universal principle, which Kohlberg identified with justice.

It is also a period of crisis for the person as he grows; the
child has reached what I call the second great mental
revolution—the ability to think and reason almost purely
verbally and to push verbal reasoning to all sorts of logical
conclusions. I refer to it as the second great moral revolution in thinking ability because the adolescent mind ex-
plodes with possibilities characterized by idealism, self-
reflection, and growth of mental abilities.[87] Good, for the
adolescent, characteristically takes on a universal character—everyone *must* be fed, or the monk is the *only* true
Christian, or all war must stop now. Because something can
be conceived, it can be accomplished! Such is the tyranny of
the adolescent mind which haunts the development of
autonomous morality.

The mind opens up endless possibilities for the early teen;
endless possibilities, however, often produce confusion, the
search for simple answers, and the absolutization of hypo-
thetical and deductive reasoning. This creates many problems for the home and the Church, since both Church and
family as institutions, as authorities, come into question as
do their value systems; the same sort of questioning characterizes the adolescent's relationships with all past associations. These questioning students have the ability now to
move into a post-conventional, autonomous, principled
level of moral reasoning. This does not mean they will reject
Christian morality or principles, but that their relationship
to them will, even must, change, as they make, or fail to
make, these values their *own*.

The cognitive development which characterizes the adolescent makes stages 5 and 6 possible, but not necessary. It is the growing sense of self and personhood, concepts developed earlier in this book, which is the prerequisite for genuine moral development in the Christian sense. Unless object-centered relationships are outgrown and rejected, we cannot speak of a moral or a spiritual person.[88] Personhood, in turn, is the foundation for community, while individuality (objectivism) is the basis for the collective.[89]

Stage 5: Social Contract Orientation. Correct action is defined in terms of what is good for the group and in terms of standards which are independent the group. In this context law is utilitarian, and when it ceases to serve the group or does harm to the rights of people, it can be rejected or violated. The U.S., and constitutional democracies in general, work at this level. Since free agreement and contractual relationships are important for the functioning of the social unit and the production of the common good, rules can be changed to benefit the society. Outside of the realm of law, determining right and wrong is a personal matter. A specific moral system is relative and subject to a larger or higher principle, a point which Christians find congenial in discussing the relationship between Gospel and law.

Most adults, particularly those in authority, have a difficult time allowing younger people to move beyond stage three and four and to question the traditional authority of the Church in moral matters. It is a happy fact that the Church has not been defined as "authority" and that both the doctrine and the structure of the Orthodox ecclesiology are relatively open. The fact remains, however, that questioning and challenging is the path to moral maturity and renewed commitment to the faith in keeping with a more mature personal development. The problem for parents, priests, and teachers is that this often involves a *values* conflict, the most difficult type of conflict for most adults to face.

This stage does not allow the breaking of law, but if it is broken then the consequence must be accepted. Individuals may not nullify legal judgment because the social system would not be able to contine. A Stage 5 response to the Heinz dilemma might be: "Heinz has to maintain his relationship with his wife and with society. If he steals as a last resort, that would meet his responsibility to his wife even though he may technically have offended society." On the other hand, "The druggist is not without fault, since he put excessive profit ahead of human welfare. The life of people can only be protected by Heinz's stealing the drug." Thus we see that in Kohlberg's system the same principles can produce different conclusions.

Stage 6: Universal Moralizing Principle Orientation. Although Kohlberg identifies this moral principle with "justice," we shall consider only the category and not the content here; we may exchange the principle of justice with a universalizing love of the Gospel. At Stage 6, right is defined as an abstract principle which is self-determined and subject to no endorsement; it exists apart from society and even apart from the person maintaining it and his self interest. The person is obliged to act according to principles, even against his own good and the good of society. The appeal is to a higher law of conscience or to a divine law which transcends the customs and laws of the community. They are not concrete rules, such as the ten commandments, but generalized principles such as human dignity, human equality, the sacredness of all life. A person acting against something he knows to be virtuous would be eventually self-destructive in Kohlberg's system as well as Christian anthropology.

Stage 6 is the level at which, in Kohlberg's analysis, the individual is self-disciplined and autonomous. I conclude that among Christians it is characterized by an unconditional faith in God and a sense of Galatian freedom of action (Galatians 4:22-5:4). Kohlberg's sixth stage is Kantian, each human being respected in, of, and for himself. Human beings cannot be reduced to ciphers or mere means to an end. The individual must never be used in a manner that is degrading or that violates him. Although unverbalized, a categorical imperative is here at play and no detailed definition is offered by Kohlberg.

St Symeon the New Theologian, St Anthony of the Desert, St Maximus the Confessor, and St Athanasius *contra mundi*—all personalities capable of standing on their own with what they knew to be true, all were conscious only of their personal relationship with God as normative. At Stage 6, a solution to the Heinz dilemma *might* be: "Heinz should steal the drug because a human life takes precedence over any moral or legal code or value. A human life has inherent value whether or not it is valued by the society or a particular individual."

Kohlberg's schema provides a convenient outline for discussing moral development and becomes useful to parents, pastors, and teachers when Christian reflections are added. He is updating aspects of it and even reconsidering what many consider an essentially unworkable Stage 6.[90] Each particular stage says nothing about the actual content of the conclusion a person may reach. Exposure to rules and principles, whether in a didactic situation or in everyday life by example, is essential.[91] It does not limit the subject's freedom to exercise his thinking capacity; it merely gives him the data with which to face a Kohlbergian dilemma. All of the criticism of the "cognitive development" approach to moral education offers the same fuzzy methods and approaches as does Kohlberg's affirmations. What is clear is that any single approach is insufficient and no one will become moral by merely being encouraged to think morally; but even to think morally he must have the mental tools and raw material to allow the moral potential at each stage to surface. Rules without the reasoning process to allow their application, and the reasoning process without the data provided by some sort of exposure to values held by the community, make morality a disconnected "game of chance."

The criticisms of cognitive moral development as an approach to teaching moral reasoning skills are applied to its use in public school and not to their application in a morally structured setting, e.g., the church school. I believe the application of a neutral process in a principled situation is embodied in John Wilson's insight.

> It is not sufficient that a person should give money to the poor, or refrain from stealing. . . for he might do all these for inadequate, or even disreputable, reasons. . . . He must act and feel for the right reasons. He cannot do this unless and until he knows what the right reasons are, and has convinced himself that they are; and he cannot get to know this unless somebody teaches it to him.[92]

The point is that in any meaningful moral development exercise, whether cognitive or affective, the student can only bring to it what is accessible to him. When Piaget affirms that a child develops morally through interaction with his environment, he is stating the obvious because the environment may well be either a cognitive dilemma, a genuine dilemma, a noteworthy person, or his parents' expectations. Ideas and principles affirmed to the child do not encourage morality, except in the case of their affirmation by a significant adult or a significant number of adults in the child's life. Even for Kohlberg, it is a process that is a process that is conditionable, depending upon more than the maturation of the human organism. There is no innate moral capacity which develops without law or socialization or relationships. It is rather for Piaget a two-fold process of assimilation and accommodation. People can take in the outside environment, but it only becomes significant when they fit it into what already exists in their makeup acquired either from experience or development. Accommodation occurs when the child puts his own stamp on the materials; the stamp may be what he knows and experiences outside of innate tendencies.[93]

Lawrence Kohlberg's schema of moral development, as well as the various techniques associated with it, generate varied responses. Many church groups have endorsed them for use in church schools, and one can find articles in the Protestant-sponsored *Church Teacher* encouraging the use of Kohlberg. On the other hand, the secular *American Teacher* rejects the use of the same techniques.[95] Some critics caricature the current batch of moral education programs as relativistic, based on the absence of right and wrong, because "to teach any substantive ethical precept is to 'indoctrinate' students."[96] Specifically referring to Kohlberg's "dilemma" approach, one critic notes that students "are asked to dwell on ethical dilemmas such as when lying can be justified...." Many educators appear to hold that the very discussion of options implies moral relativity. Certainly, the fact that a teacher allows a spectrum of values to be expressed, each having equal validity from a cognitive or methodological point of view, does not endorse those values, especially if the objective of the method is teaching how to reason morally. In fact, we have been confronted by the problem of American pluralism turned from specific values transmission to the supposedly neutral process of *valuing* and *moral thinking*. I do not believe this to be so deadly as do Westerhoff and others such as James Dobson.[97] Westerhoff notes that he doubts the problems from Kohlberg or Simon will benefit the moral development of our youth.[98] He focuses on the single weakest aspect of Kohlbergian technique—"how are the values transmitted?" In Westerhoff, the process of valuing has replaced values. I see no such conflict necessary in Kohlberg and, in fact, see Westerhoff creating a "straw man." The process of clarifying values or analyzing dilemmas does not preclude having values, and, perchance, even strongly held values!

We, however, must affirm that moral issues unlike moral principles are often not "black and white." Eastland notes that the main problem, and with this I must agree, is that this technique leaves the emotions untouched. No one is taught to have evil and to love the truth! "Today's 'moral education' fails in the most critical way because it addresses the intellect but not the emotions. No one is taught to dislike and certainly not to hate anything."[99] The fact that Eastland can with justification claim that "the craze in the schools today is a type of 'moral education' that is unfortunately empty of substantive morality" is not the problem of the technique; it is the problem of a society that has lost its moral nerve.[100] In keeping with this line of criticism, William Bennett sarcastically notes:

> A moral educationist's model moral person is one who is always in doubt, in dilemma, tearing his hair out, to get clear about what to do. The moral individual, however, is rarely presented as a conscientious person, a person of character and equanimity, who, because of his character, doesn't have to face hard choices every ten minutes or every ten days.[101]

This is an overstated, albeit valid, criticism; the fact remains that people do discuss their options when options exist. Howard Kirschenbaum in his *Advanced Value Clarification* writes:

> What about discipline, Professor Kirschenbaum?

> Supposing a fight breaks out in class. Do we do values clarification? Is that the student's free choice? Kirschenbaum answers, "Not in my classroom. Nor is cheating or ridiculing others allowed in my classroom. I put a stop to those right away. I do not pretend that that is values clarification. This is discipline.[102]

One of the main criticisms of Kohlberg's approach is the lack of actual moral focus, the lack of traditional teaching by example and precept. As we have already noted, moral development is multifaceted—behavioral, psychoanalytic, and cognitive. Moral content is communicated by the community through the very structure of its life. From a specifically Christian perspective, morality cannot be restricted to justice as the ultimate principle. Do Christians follow principles of justice or the person of Christ? Christians' moral response derives from a relationship with God and the desire to become like him and share in his life (II Peter 2:4). "The Kingdom of God comes in and disrupts conclusions made on a purely cognitive basis. The point here is that faith perspective actually alters the form of moral thinking, not only the content"[103] Faith cannot be reduced to belief, as Kohlberg has done when he concludes that religion plays no demonstrable role in moral judgment.[104] The decisive difference between his Stage 6 (Universal Moralizing Principle Orientation) and Christian morality based on the reality of the Kingdom cannot be ignored even as I affirm the value of the techniques he employs. Justice is rooted in the person of Jesus Christ, not in an abstract principle or idea.

The problem we face as an established and institutional Church is how to allow discussion on already decided issues of either doctrine or morality—war, peace, abortion, Trinity, theosis, and so on. Are these open to discussion? Yes! As an educational effort, everything is open to discussion.

Sophie Koulomzin describes in a short passage of her book, *Many Worlds: A Russian Life*, the need to permit younger people the opportunity to work out solutions, even if incorrect. Writing of her youth discussion group in Estonia and the guidance of Father John Bogoyavlensky's care for the group, she says:

> Not only did he take the trouble to sit courteously, attentively and silently through the adult Bible classes taught by Mr. Gott, but he seemed to remain completely unshaken by our weird discussions. I remember that one day we set up a so-called "Literary Court of Justice," based on the story "Judas Iscariot" by Leonid Andreev, and somehow, to our own horror, finished up with a verdict of "not guilty." Father John's trust in us, his refusal to condemn us as heretics, or preach at us, was amazing. Even now I am not sure on what it was based.[105]

Educational Uses

Kohlberg's educational theory is based on the "stimulation" of moral development.[106] Kohlberg's techniques of moral education, like Socrates' dialogue method, were designed to create a "dissatisfaction" within the student by exposing him to moral conflicts for which he does not yet have a solution. What is essential, I believe, is to understand that Kohlberg's techniques imply a social process in which the person is exposed to his peers' and teachers' disagreement and argument about a moral issue. A person does not move from one stage to the next without interaction, be it in the family, classroom, or parish youth group. It is the interaction that provides the cognitive dissonance. This dissonance may be stimulated by an airing of differing opinions, viewing a movie (e.g., "Ghandi", "Officer and a Gentleman"), studying the life of a saint, or reading the Scriptures.

Kohlberg and his fellow researchers experimented with

various types of moral intervention, planned educational activity, which might affect the rate of a person's moral development. Kohlberg uses his dilemmas as "pacers" to stimulate reflection and facilitate development.[107] The one found to be most effective was a moral dilemma discussion program, which enabled the majority of persons participating to advance to a higher level of moral *reasoning*.[108] (The reasoning process was the area most easily controlled and measured.) Attempting to resolve a dilemma by being exposed to differing opinions, the students may be forced to go to a stage higher than his predominant stage to solve the dilemma. John Elias has noted: "I believe that his case study approach is well suited to do this, for it affords the person opportunity to confront moral reasoning at a higher level than his own."[109] Such a process was not unknown to the early Fathers as quoted above.

Stimulation to a higher level of thinking occurs only if the person changes his form of thinking about the dilemma. The educator encourages development by promoting cognitive dissonance or disequilibrium, that is, by presenting a moral dilemma in such a way that the student will not be able to satisfactorily resolve the dilemma with his current reasoning skills.[110]

How does an educator promote cognitive dissonance? The group leader must first assess the students' level of moral reasoning by questioning them about a specific issue that involves a conflict between two drives, as between law and human life, in order to uncover their moral presuppositions. The reasoning behind the students' proposed solutions, not the solutions themselves, indicate their level of moral "maturity" or their stage. Second, the educator selects and supports an argument that is one stage above the majority stage of thinking. It is hoped that through exposure to a higher level of reasoning, students will see the inconsistencies and inadequacies of their own stage and then move to a higher stage in order to resolve the contradictions in the reasoning process proposed by the students themselves. It is Kohlberg's presupposition that people tend to prefer higher to lower stages as long as they are not so much higher that they cannot understand them; they prefer one or two stages, but not more, above their currect one. Another effective method is for the educator to have higher stage individuals point out the weaknesses of lower stage conclusions. Any book on Kohlberg will outline techniques that can be used with his theory, but ultimately, the starting point is to listen to where the students are.

The classroom-discussion program is but one example of how the cognitive-developmental approach can be applied in the church school or the home. The classroom discussion approach should be part of a broader, more enduring involvement of students in the school's functioning.[111] In addition to actual moral intervention, it is important for someone with a socialization model to point out that Kohlberg also stresses the importance of the institution for the individual. If the school operates at stage one (the administration makes all the rules and the students must obey or be punished), it is difficult for students to see the advantage of operating above stages 1 or 2.[112]

Evaluation

Let us stand back and evaluate the strengths and weaknesses of Kohlberg's approach. His emphasis on the person as an active subject, a knower, more than a passive recipient of moral imperatives, is essentially positive, and his pacer technique allows the student to call upon data from his own experience or education. In this approach, morality is more than the internalization of social, political, or ecclesiastical values; it is the person accommodating his environment in a dynamic manner, with the emphasis on the agent as responsible and answerable for decisions which he is obliged to explain as part of the process.

Kohlberg holds that behavior is an expression of reasoning; he is weak, however, on the connection between moral thinking and moral behavior, and he minimizes an approach based on judging behavior, believing such an approach to be inadequate to the human mind and personality development. Morality for Kohlberg is cheapened by reducing it to the reinforcement of "good behavior." He ignores the interplay of behavior and belief and thus does not treat the internal dynamic, the will, the enabling factors that motivate a person to do what he has judged to be correct in a given situation. He has said, for instance, that "the man who understands justice is more likely to practice it."[113] Why is this the case and what in his mind empowers people to act according to what they understand as right? Moral judgment does not translate automatically into moral action. Ethical behavior, unlike ethical thinking, is a multifaceted reality which for Christians cannot be understood adequately apart from the empowering strength of Christ.

Turning again to the strengths of his approach, we must include his affirmation of the mysterious notion of conscience, by which a person makes decisions at Stage 6. His treatment of the person as moral agent allows the teachers or pastor to treat the age as a group, so we can speak of a child-centered morality and an adult-centered morality. By extension, moral development does not end with adolescence, and Kohlberg's methods are as useful with adults as with children. Finally, he is concerned with the environment, and the establishment of what he calls a "just structure" to be reflected in the educational setting calls for the reduction of inconsistencies in our systems.

Although the cognitive-developmental approach has

proven effective in raising a person's level of moral thinking, this does not prove that a formalistic model of ethics is a sufficient ethical model. The Orthodox must ask whether morality is more than a rational process. Clearly it is; it has a primary affective component which cannot be reduced to processes, but falls within the category of behaviorized socialization. We know this and we know that children learn what they see lived, by being told, and by being related to in certain manners. Teaching morality by moralizing, by example, and by treatment is not negated by the affirmation of cognitive techniques. We cannot, of course, accept Kohlberg's approach in its neutral or relativistic implication. We can and should use Kohlberg's techniques for heightening moral awareness and thinking processes. Moral development must occur on the behavioral, psychoanalytical (socialization), and developmental planes, and the meeting point is the Christian community that seeks to educate and shape a learning environment for its people.

Chapter 4 Footnotes

[1]Stanley Harakas, *Contemporary Moral Issues Facing the Orthodox Christian* (Minneapolis: Light and Life Publishing, 1982).

[2]George W. Forell, *History of Christian Ethics*, Vol. I (Minneapolis: Augsburg Publishing House, 1979), 120, best develops these themes. Eric Osborn, *Ethical Patterns in Early Christian Thought* (Cambridge: Cambridge University Press, 1978), 120, however, is better for the fourth-century Fathers and more attuned to the theological elements of Basil, for instance, and the centrality of *mutualism* in his monastic rule.

[3]See Lawrence Kohlberg, "Stages of Moral Development as a Basis for Moral Education," in C.M. Beck *et al, Moral Education: Interdisciplinary Approaches* (Toronto: University of Toronto Press, 1971) 86-88; Kohlberg, "Cognitive-Developmental Approach to Moral Education," *The Humanist*, Vol. 15, (November-December, 1972). Perhaps the clearest statement of his belief in a Platonic goal to moral development is found in his 1974 presentation to the National Catholic Educational Association, "Education, Moral Development, and Faith," *Journal of Moral Education*, 4 (1974), 5-16.

[4]Ronald Duska and Mariellen Whelen, *A Guide to Piaget and Kohlberg* (New York: Paulist Press, 1975), is perhaps the best popular, readable introduction to both Jean Piaget and Lawrence Kohlberg.

[5]James Fowler, the last of the developmental quartet, is still formulating his application of Piaget to faith development. The entire issue, however, seems problematic, due to the very nature of faith as to make many Christians uneasy. Using Piaget's cognitive schema he centers faith on process as opposed to content; faith for Fowler, is verbified, *faithing*, whose form does not determine the quality of the process. See James Fowler, *Stages of Faith: The Psychology of Human Development and the Quest for Meaning* (New York: Harper and Row, 1981), Part I. See also James Fowler and Sam Keen, *Life Maps: Conversations on the Journey of Faith* (Minneapolis: Winston Press, 1978), for a dialogue on Fowler's approach.

[6]Clement of Alexandria, *Stomata* 1.6 in *Ante-Nicene Fathers* series, Vol. 2, (New York: Charles Scribner's Sons, 1926), 307. On the other hand, Basil affirms the stoic belief that virtues exist in us also by nature; the soul has an affinity with them not by education but by nature itself. Nature will support the rules he outlines as well as the sacraments. See Basil, Hexaemeron 9.4 in *Nicene and Post-Nicene Fathers*, Vol. 8, series two (Grand Rapids, MI: Eerdmans, 1955), 103. John Chrysostom tends to agree and speaks of virtues as being self-taught. See *Concerning the Statues*, Homily 12, 9 in *Nicene and Post-Nicene Fathers*, series two (Grand Rapids, MI: Eerdmans, 1956), Vol. 9, series 1, 421. For a treatment of the relationship among heredity, environment, and grace, see Elias Matsagourias, *The Early Church Fathers as Educators* (Minneapolis, MN: Light and Life Publishing, 1977), 33-45.

[7]Forell, *op.cit., passim* and Osborn, *op.cit., passim*. Both Forell and Osborn attempt to systematize the ethical teachings of the Fathers of the first four centuries. Each manages to demonstrate a different approach for the same Fathers, which makes their tandem use so fruitful. Forell is more closely tied to patterns unique to each father, as Clement of Alexandria focusing on "sins of the flesh," for instance. Osborn, on the other hand, works all the Fathers into the themes of Righteousness, Discipleship, Faith, and Love. One thing is clear: the pagan writers and philosophers played a significant role in the pattern and content of early Christian ethical thinking.

[8]See above, "Growing Into Community," Chapter 2.

[9]Gregory Nazianzen, *In Defence of His Flight to Pontus*, in *Nicene and Post-Nicene Fathers*, series two, Vol. 7 (Grand Rapids, MI: Eerdmans, 1974), chapter 21, 209.

[10]B.F. Skinner, *Beyond Freedom and Dignity*, (New York: A. Knopf, 1971), 10.

[11]John L. Elias, *Psychology and Religious Education* (Bethlehem, PA: Catechetical Communications, 1975), 18.

[12]Skinner, *op.cit.*; John R. Moz, "Flannery O'Connor: Southerner and Catholic," *New Catholic World*, 224 (Nov-Dec 1981), 261-267.

[13]Origen maintains in his *Contra Celsum* a clear ethical teaching; he accepts those who become Christians out of the fear of punishment for sin or reward for good works because their former lives would have forced them further from God. For him, even behavior modification can occasion a renewed judgment and insight. See *Contra Celsum* in *Ante-Nicene Fathers*, Vol. 4, (New York: Charles Scribner's Sons, 1926), 400.

[14]For example, Canons of Council of Elvira in Spain, (c.309). For the problem of treating sexual offenses, see Forell, *op.cit.*, 102. He concludes that the emphasis on offenses, especially so-called hidden ones, reflect an historic development of a strong and centralized ecclesiastical leadership. *Ibid.*, 8.

[15]St. John Chrysostom, *Baptismal Instructions*, in the *Nicene and Post-Nicene Fathers*, series one, Vol. 9 (New York: Christian Literature Co., 1889), 159-179.

[16]Gregory Nazianzen, *In Defense*, chapter 33, 211.

[17]See for example Helen Waddell, *The Desert Fathers* (Ann Arbor, MI: University of Michigan Press, 1960), 114, 123.

[18]Gregory Nazianzen, *In Defense*, chapter 45, 214.

[19]Lukas Vischer, "Introduction in the Life of Faith in the Early Church," *Risk*, II (1st Quarter, 1966), 42-44, on the role of moral elements of catechumenate. See more recently, Richard Connaly, *Didascalia Apostolorum: The Syriac Version Translated, Accompanied by the Verona Latin Fragments* (Oxford: Clarendon Press, 1969), 147ff.

[20]See above, Boojamra, "The Family as the Origin of Pre-Theological Personality Characteristics," Chapter 3.

[21]C.S. Lewis, *Mere Christianity* (New York: Macmillan Company, 1958), 100-101.

[22]Paul Lehmann, *Ethics in a Christian Context* New York: Harper and Row, 1963), 59.

[23]See a workbook adaptation of Kohlberg in Ronald Galbraith and Thomas Jones, *Moral Reasoning* (Minneapolis: Greenhaven Press Inc., 1976); also Susan Pagliuso, *Understanding Stages of Moral Development* (New York: Paulist Press, 1976).

[24]Rudolph Bultmann, *Glauben and Verstehen: Gesammelte Aufsatze*, 234-235; quoted in Forell, *op.cit.*, 21.

[25]Origen, *Contra Celsum* 1.9, 400.

[26]Basil of Caesarea, Letter 2, in *Saint Basil, The Letters*, I, translated by R. Deferrari, Loeb Classical Library (New York: Putnam, 1926), 15.

[27]See *Ibid.*, Letter 2, for instance, where Job is the model of fortitude.

[28]Basil of Caesarea, *The Morals*, 80,1 translated by W.K.L. Clarke (London: SPCK, 1925), 127.

[29]Gregory Nazianzen, *Oration on the Occasion of the Funeral of Basil the Great*, chapter 12 in *Nicene and Post-Nicene Fathers*, Vol. 7, series 2 (Grand Rapids: Eerdmans, 1974, reprint), 399. On modeling, one author notes that when a child, even unintentionally, imitates another 'as members of a group, do to take over each other's mode of behavior and thereby form common habits." See Ruth Berenda, "The Influence of the Group on the Development of Children," in Morris and Natalie Haimowitz (eds.) *Human Development* (New York: Thomas Rowell Co., 1963), 327-353, at 343. Also on modeling, Albert Bondman, "Social Learning through Imitation," in M.R. Jones (ed.) *Nebraska Symposium on Motivation* (Lincoln, NB: University of Nebraska Press, 1962). The trustworthy nature, pleasant disposition of the model, enhances the model in the mind of the child; Albert Bondman and A. Huston, "Identification as a Process of Incidental Learning," in *Journal of Abnormal Social Psychology*, 63(1961), 311-318.

[30]Forell, *op.cit.*, 28.

[31]Gregory Nazianzen, *In Defense*, chapter 15, 208.

[32]Clement of Alexandria, *Stromateis*, 2.22, 131.5 in *Ante-Nicene Fathers*, Vol. 4 (Edinburgh, 1882, 1884). See also Eric Osborn *The Philosophy of Clement of Alexandria* (Cambridge: Cambridge University Press, 1957), 89.

[33]See Zachary Xintaras, "Man—The Image of God According to Greek Fathers," *Greek Orthodox Theological Review*, I (August, 1954), 48-62.

[34]Basil of Caesarea, *Letter CCXXXIII*, in *Nicene and Post-Nicene Fathers*, series two, Vol. 7 (Grand Rapids, MI: 1955), 273.

[35]John Chirban, *Human Growth and Faith: Intrinsic and Extrinsic Motivation in Human Development* (Washington, DC: University Press of America, 1981), 95-119.

[36]John of Damascus, *Exposition of the Orthodox Faith*, in *Nicene and Post-Nicene Fathers*, series two, Vol. 12 (Grand Rapids, MI: Eerdmans 1956) Book 2, Ch 12, 31-32. Also see Ephesians 4:13 and II Peter 1:4.

[37]John Meyendorff, "Significance of the Reformation in the History of Christendom," in *Catholicity and the Church* (Crestwood, NY: St. Vladimir's Seminary Press, 1983), 74-75.

[38]Clement of Alexandria, *The Instructor*, III, Chapter 1, 271. Also Isaac the Syrian, quoted in Chairton of Valaam, *The Art of Prayer*, translated by Kadloubovsky and Palmer (London: Faber and Faber, 1967), 164.

[39]Gregory Nazianzen, *In Defense*, chapter 44, 214.

[40]*Ibid.*, chapter 48, 215.

[41]Gregory Nazianzen, *In Defense*, chapter 45, 214.

[42]*Ibid.*

[43]See Forell, *op.cit.*, 26-29: "The Deviant Functioning of the Mind."

[44]See the brilliant works of Lucie Barber, *Celebrating the Second Year of Life* (Birmingham, AL: Religious Education Press, 1978), 116-117 and Lucie Barber, *The Religious Education of Preschool Children* (Birmingham, AL: Religious Education Press, 1981), 46-47, 61-62.

[45]Richard Reichert, "Do They Know How Good They Really Are?" in Robert Heyer (ed.), *The Religious Life of the Adolescent* (New York: Paulist Press, 1974), 16-23.

[46]Jean Piaget, *The Moral Judgment of the Child* (New York: The Free Press, 1965), 376.

[47]Erik Erikson, *Identity: Youth and Crisis* (New York: Norton, 1968).

[48]Reichert, *op.cit.*, 18.

[49]See the foundational classic, Erik Erikson, *Childhood and Society* (New York: Norton, 1950).

[50]Jean Piaget, *The Moral Judgment.*

[51]Kohlberg, "Moral Education in the Schools: A Developmental View," *School Review*, 74 (1966), 1-30.

[52]See Erikson, *op.cit.*, 70, where he refers to the deadliest of all sins as the destruction of the child's spirit, particularly his sense of trust, autonomy, initiative, and industry. Also for an interpretative lecture, see Joseph Allen, "Christian Personality Development" in J. L. Boojamra (ed.), *Teaching Dynamic* (Englewood, NJ: Department of Christian Education, 1978), Tape 3, Side 2.

[53]Erik Erikson, *The Young Man Luther* (New York: Norton, 1958), 20-21, and Erikson, *Childhood and Society* (New York: Norton, 1950), 250. I will try to integrate Erikson's foundational categories into Kohlberg's schema. Fuller treatment can be found above in "The Christian Family as the Basis of Pre-Theological Development," Chapter 3.

[54]Gordon Allport, *The Nature of Prejudice* (Reading, MA: Addison-Wesley, 1954).

[55]Duska and Whelan, *op.cit.*, 5-41.

[56]*Ibid.*, 42-45.

[57]Duska and Whelan, *op.cit.*, 8. Also see L. Kohlberg and P. Turiel, "Moral Development and Moral Education," in G. Lesser (ed.), *Psychology and Educational Practice* (New York: Scot, Foresman, 1971), 415.

[58]There is great misplaced emphasis on so-called new-era child rearing in which children are treated as equals, sharing in parental burdens and problems. On the danger of the democratization of child-rearing see Marie Winn, *Children Without Childhood* (New York: Pantheon Books, 1983), 45-56; and Vance Packard, *Our Endangered Children* (Boston: Little, Brown, and Co., 1983), 111-134.

[59]Bruno Bettelheim, "Education and the Reality Principle," *American Educator*, 3(Winter, 1979), 11.

[60]*Ibid.*

[61]*Ibid.*, notes that Piaget's work is or may be conditioned by his Genevese location with its middle class culture and relatively stable society. In America he notes heteronomity may be limited by the fact that peers play a greater role earlier in life. "The parents become less and less domineering in the child's life, the relations between the parent and the child less unilateral...." He notes the early entrance into nursery school in the United States as one reason for this. The possible conclusion to this in Piaget's terms is that children learn the morality of cooperation earlier. This author is not sure how significant this factor is given the fact of the very size of the parents and the developmental limitations on the assimilation of experiences.

[62]For example, see Osborn, *op.cit.*, 103; and Forell, *op.cit.*, 126, 148-149.

[63]Kohlberg, "Moral Education," 3-5.

[64]See above, "Socialization as an Historical Model of Christian Integration," Chapter 2.

[65]Kohlberg, "Moral Education," 1-30. Elias, *op.cit.*, 67-68.

[66]Lawrence Kohlberg, "Stages of Moral Development as a Basis for Moral Education,"in C.M. Beck (ed.), *Moral Education: Interdisciplinary Approaches* (Toronto: University of Toronto, 1971), 85-88.

[67]Winn, *op.cit.*, 97 "But underlying [Freud's] insights is a fatalistic assumption of an essential identity between children and adults that allows their behavior to be interpreted according to the same standards. See also the observations of Constance Tarasar, " 'Taste and See': Orthodox Children at Worship," in Diane Apostolos-Cappadona (ed.), *The Sacred Play of Children* (New York: The Seabury Press, 1983), 43-54, at 44.

[68]Lawrence Kohlberg, "From Is to Ought and How to Commit the Naturalistic Fallacy and Get Away With It in the Study of Moral Development," in T. Mischel (ed.), *Cognitive Development and Epistemology* (New York: Academic Press, 1971), 215.

[69]Lawrence Kohlberg, "The Cognitive-Developmental Approach to Moral Education," in Peter Scharf, *et al* (eds.), *Readings in Moral Education* (Minneapolis: Winston Press, 1978), 37-39.

[70]Gregory Nazianzen, for instance, notes in his *Defense of His Flight*, 214, the learning differences due to ages among people.

[71]Cicero, *De Officiis*, III, 28, translated by Walter Miller (New York: Putnam, 1928), 17. Kohlberg himself claims that his cognitive-developmental approach has its origin in Socrates' Athens. See Lawrence Kohlberg, "Forward," to Peter Scharf (ed.), *Readings in Moral Education* (Minneapolis: Winston Press, 1978), 9. See John Wilson and Barbara Cowell, *Dialogues on Moral Education* (Birmingham, AL: Religious Education Press, 1983), for a treatment of the Socratic model.

[72]Ambrose of Milan, *Duties of the Clergy*, in *Nicene and Post-Nicene Fathers*, series two, Vol. X (Grand Rapids, MI: Eerdmans, 1955), Book III, Ch 4, 107.

[73]Quoted in Peter Scharf, *Moral Education* (Davis, CA: Responsible Action, 1978), 47.

[74]See chapters 2 and 3.

[75]See for outline of Piaget's categories, Scharf, *Moral Education*, 36-39. See also David Wickens, "Pedagogical Principles Derived from Piaget's Theory," in Milton Schwebel and Jane Raph (eds.), *Piaget in the Classroom* (New York: Basic Books, 1973), chapter 9.

[76]For the best introduction to Piaget's description of mental operations, see Barry Wadsworth, *Piaget's Theory of Cognitive Development* (New York: Longman, 1971), 74-75, 92-93. Also Hermina Sinclair, "Recent Piagetian Research in Learning Studies," in Schwebel, *op.cit.*, 57-72.

[77]Duska and Whelan, *op.cit.*, 9-13; also Barber, *Religious Education*, 30, 32.

[78]Duska and Whelan, *op.cit.*, 7-13.

[79]See the role of community for Orthodox theology and anthropology in chapters 1 and 2.

[80]Wadsworth, *op.cit.*, 73-75, where it is discussed in terms of *transformation* and *centering*. Fowler makes reference to "perspective taking" as part of faith development. See Fowler, *Life Maps*, 60-61.

[81]Selma Fraiberg, *Every Child's Birthright* (New York: Basic Books, 1977), 27, 45. Also Packard, *op.cit.*, 129-131.

[82]On the danger of privatism, see chapter above. See also Fred Hechinger, "Can Morality Be Taught?" *New York Times*, July 8, 1979, c1, c4.

[83]Philip Greven, *The Protestant Temperament* (New York: Alfred A. Knopf, 1980), 46-48.

[84]Elias, *op.cit.*, 39. See Jean Marzollo and Janice Lloyd, *Learning Through Play* (New York: Harper and Row, 1972), 2-3. Winn, *op.cit.*, 75-80. Although an age for the so-called "first confession" is not discussed, there is a reference in Balsamon, (1105-1195), The Canonist, in which he comments on Timotheos' *Canonical Answers*; Balsamon notes that no particular age is set because it depends on the nature of the child. See Rhalles and Pottle, *Syntagma ton Theion kai Ieron Kanonon* IV (Athens,), 341.

[85]Lawrence Kohlberg, "Moral Development from the Standpoint of General Psychological Theory," in Thomas Lickona (ed.), *Moral Development and Behavior: Theory, Research, and Social Issues* (New York: Holt, Rinehart, and Winston, 1976), 50.

[86]Elias, *op.cit.*, 47.

[87]Ronald Goldman, *Religious Thinking From Childhood to Adolescence* (New York: The Seabury Press, 1964), 239-246. See Merton P. Strommen, *Five Cries of Youth* (New York: Harper and Row, 1979), 52-71.

[88]Reichert, *op.cit.*, 19-20.

[89]On the theological notion of Christian *personhood*, see above, Chapter 3.

[90]On the difficulty of working with Stage 6, see the critical treatment of Kevin Walsh and Milly Cowles, *Developmental Discipline* (Birmingham, AL: Religious Education Press, 1982), 230, note 17, where Kohlberg's ten subsidiary categories of justice are discussed. Kohlberg toys with a Stage 7 tied to religious categories due to his sense of the inadequacy of Stage 6. See Lawrence Kohlberg and Clark Power, "Moral Development, Religious Thinking, and the Question of a Seventh Stage," in *Zygon*, XVI (September, 1981), 203-259.

[91]See Lawrence Kohlberg, "Adult Moral Development" (New York: Reference on Adult Religious Education, Religious Education Association, 1976), tape #10, where he speaks of a metaphorical stage seven in which love is primary.

[92]A term applied by William Bennett and Edwin Delatre, "A Moral Education," *American Educator*, 3 (Winter, 1979), 8, to caricature the cognitive development approach.

[93]John Wilson, *Pratical Methods of Moral Education* (London: Heinemann Educational Books, 1972), 44.

[94]See Milton Schwebel and Jane Raph, (eds.), *Piaget in the Classroom* (New York: Basic Books, 1973), 111-112, 127.

[95]Norman Beck, "Why Should We Have Church Schools?" *Church School*, Vol. (July-August, 1982), 8-10. Opposed to this is Bennett and Delatre, *op.cit.*, 6-9. See the critical rejection of values and cognitive-developmental education in James Dobson, *Dare to Discipline* (New York: Bantam Books, 1978).

[96]For example, see Terry Eastland, "Teaching Morality in Public Schools," *The Wall Street Journal*, February 22, 1981, 1.

[97]See John H. Westerhoff III, *Will Our Children Have Faith?* (New York: Seabury Press, 1976), 19-20 where he chastizes the religious education community for giving itself to the behavioral sciences, including development psychology, and ignoring the socialization process.

[98]He has shifted to issues of faith in *Will Our Children Have Faith* as the basis for moral development. Recently returned to values with some new insights. In a topical lecture, from the Religious Education Association, "Values for Today's Children," (REA International Convention, Toronto, 1979), tape #21.

[99]*Ibid.*, 1.

[100]Eastland, *op.cit.*, 1.

[101]William Bennett, "What Value is Values Education," *American Educator*, 4 (Fall, 1980), 31.

[102]Quoted in *Ibid.*, 32.

[103]Zappone, *op.cit.*, 115.

[104]Elias, *op.cit.*, 66. Kohlberg has concluded that religious background has little to do with stages in moral reasoning. He has found no important distinction in the moral reasoning of Catholics, Protestants, Muslims, etc. He, however, seems to confuse religious faith with affiliation.

[105]Sophie Koulomzin, *Many Worlds: A Russian Life* (Crestwood, NY: St Vladimir's Seminary Press, 1980).

[106]Kohlberg, "From Is to Ought," 183.

[107]James Fowler, "Stages of Faith: The Psychology of Human Development and the Quest for Meaning," reviewed by Steven Ivy in *Journal of Pastoral Care*, 36 (December, 1982), 265-274. Jane Loevinger, *Ego Development: Conceptions and Theories* (San Francisco: Jassey-Bass Pub., 1976), 308-309, suggests that therapeutic growth occurs most readily when the therapist offers "pacers which are one-half to one step ahead of the clients present developmental level."

[108]Lawrence Kohlberg and Rocelle Mayer, "Development as the Aim of Education," *Harvard Educational Review*, XLII (November, 1972), 484. Also Moshe Blatt and Lawrence Kohlberg, "The Effects of Classroom Moral Discussion Upon Children's Level of Moral Judgement," in Kohlberg and Turiel (eds.), *Recent Research in Moral Development* (New York: Holt, Rinehart, and Winston, 1973), chapter 38.

[109]Elias, *op.cit.*, 39.

[110]Duska and Whelan, *op.cit.*, chapter 4.

[111]Kohlberg, "A Cognitive-Developmental Approach to Moral Education," *The Humanist* (November-December, 1972), 16.

[112]Kohlberg, P. Scharf, and J. Hickey, "The Justice Structure of the Prison—A Theory and an intervention," *The Prison Journal*, II (Autumn-Winter, 1972), p3-13, quoted in Katherine E. Zappone, "Kohlberg for Chaplains: A Theory of Moral Development." Also, L. Kohlberg, "The Child and Moral Philosophy," *Psychology Today* (September, 1968), 20-29.

[113]Lawrence Kohlberg, "The Development of Children's Orientation Towards a Moral Order. Sequence in the Development of Moral Thought," *Vita Humana VI* (1963), 30.

CHAPTER 5

Conclusions

Any field needs intellectual foundations from which to operate and plan for future changes. Orthodox Christian education is no exception. It requires a body of knowledge which transcends the limited experience of its practitioners—in this case pastors, parents, and teachers. Without these foundations they will not know what they want to achieve or be able to establish criteria by which to judge their success or failure.[1] Anyone attempting to engage in Christian education at any level of the parish's life should do so with the benefit of relatively new knowledge from developmental psychology, educational psychology, and a broader understanding of the nature of the Christian life. The Church must use these foundations to overcome the maladaptations, discussed in the introduction, which have come to characterize Orthodox Christian education.

In an effort to provide the foundations for planning total parish education, I have (1) ventured into an analysis of the limitations of current Christian education practices in chapter one, (2) provided a context in the unifying theme of socialization in chapter two, (3) elaborated on the socialization model with the family in chapter three in terms of pre-theological and pre-spiritual formation, and, finally, (4) in chapter four, focused on the subject—the developing person—of the educational enterprise. I have, therefore, reduced the foundations of Orthodox Christian education to the Church or community, the family or beginnings, and the person as a developing reality. There are, no doubt, other foundations. These, however, provide not only convenient points from which to begin, but also the matrix for discussion and integrating other aspects of Christian education which might arise.

The value of a systems approach to Christian education is that neither the entire learning process nor any one foundation of that process can be understood without a grasp of all three—the Church, the family, and the person—as dynamically interrelated and interacting with one another. It is in this context that I am able to reaffirm my introductory remarks that learning/teaching happens at any time, at any place, by anyone. Only when we realize this, accept this, and practice this can Christian education be placed in the context of the total parish and the total person. Education, as a systemic reality, has no unique time, no unique place, and no unique person as subject or object!

Gloria Durka of Fordham University's Graduate School of Religion and Religious Education notes that "the most important contribution graduate programs can make is to help define the theoretic esoteric knowledge which makes religious education a distinct discipline. . . ."[2] Orthodox Christian education rests on a series of theoretical and practical foundations, on a series of assumptions about the Church, the family, and the person. What we have discovered is that without these foundations we cannot determine content or set aims and determine objectives for our programs. Without objectives, without aims we cannot determine where we are going, how we will get there, or whether or not we have been successful in the enterprise.

I have developed these themes hoping to stimulate discussion among Orthodox Christian parents, priests, and educators—a discussion which will enable us to clarify exactly what we want here and now and for the future. Too often programs, materials, and or curricula are a generation away and then hopelessly outdated when instituted. We are obliged by the sheer force of our limited resources as a Church in North America to plan carefully because the process cannot easily, casually, or inexpensively be repeated. Having determined what I believe are the irreducible foundations of Church and people on which to base a viable and sound Christian education program, we then need to know how to plan for what we want to happen.

Certainly, if these foundations are to be at all useful, then it must be in terms of providing a frame of reference for proactive planning, that is, planning that is designed not on the basis of present needs (reactive), not on the basis of guesses about what the future will require (projective), but planning based on what we as Church educators want to have happen. Proactive planning enables us to seize the initiative and shape a future based on the educational foundations that the Church sets for itself, embodying the best techniques available.[3]

I have selected these foundations with the firm conviction that any education must by its very nature be a total education—education of the total person by the total parish through all aspects of its life. To plan for a partial education is to plan to distort both the person and the Church. At best, this is an injustice; at the worst, a heresy. We must as pastors, parents, and educators seek to reach total persons in all aspects of their lives—emotional, physical, and intellectual; we must reach them with the total Church factual, faithful, worshiping, serving, praying, teaching, socializing. Isolating aspect may make it easier to plan and to teach, but we must be aware that we risk distorting the process by isolating any one aspect.

Here it would be well for me to summarize some of my introductory remarks as guidelines:

1. The object of education is not the child or only children between the ages of 6 and 16. Education is directed at *people* and it is this belief which frees us from the tyranny of "childhood."

2. Education does not belong only in a classroom; it belongs wherever it can take place, wherever people can be affected, changed, or influenced meaningfully.

3. Just as all the education is not confined to the classroom, teachers are not the only educators. The entire community, beginning with the family, is educator.

4. All learning is developmentally conditioned; this is the essence of total parish, total person education. It is precisely this educational reality that makes the community as educator so foundationally important for Orthodox Christians. Interaction between the community's generations provides the living context for that faith in the person of Jesus Christ, which is our ultimate goal as Christian educators.

It is appropriate to draw some practical conclusions based on the specific foundations I have treated—community, family, personhood; this may in some way hint at the manner in which the foundations can affect what we do in a sermon, conversation, classroom, liturgy, or at the dinner table. I have already mentioned some critical conclusions to be drawn for the family's nurturing of its children and the means by which love, trust, and hope can be concretely communicated to the pre-logical person; I have also indicated in chapter four some practical conclusions for moral development in the Church and the home and specific means by which we can encourage or enhance moral development, such as group play and democrative discussion techniques. If we are to take seriously these foundations, then we must find ways to incorporate them in the work of our parish programs, materials, and methods.

The community or Church as the socializer is my first foundation, and implementing a socialization model centers on the reality of all *Christian* education being *Church* education and having as its focus, content, and context, the Church of Christ. This emphasis is not designed to separate us from a personal and living relationship with Jesus Christ, but to provide a social and ecclesial context for that relationship to become reality. There can be no Protestant retreat into Scriptures as the foundation because the Scriptures are the Church's creation; there can be no retreat into a one-to-one relation with the Lord because the one whom we relate to is the one who lives in and gives breath to that Church. The health, vitality, and congruency of the Church in its local expression is vital to the teaching ministry because we cannot teach what we cannot model. It is the first principle of Christian education that we cannot share what we do not ourselves possess. It is not so much a question of making our people Christians but of the Church's (read also family's) being Christian with and through its members. The Church's rituals, symbols, and stories—it's traditions—must be vigorous, reasonable, alive, and obvious to all, and all must have a share in them. It is as simple as kissing an icon, making a procession, partaking of the eucharist. In a Church with a no-holds-barred sense of celebration, all have traditionally had access to that celebration. All people, especially children, as baptized Christians, are full and complete members of the Church and so have access to the fullness of its life. Is the liturgical and symbolic life of the Orthodox parish reasonable? Is it sensible? Is it dramatic enough to draw the faithful into it? Are the symbolic elements clear and self-evident? Are the children encouraged to be part of all events? Are they aware of their life in the Church and the fact that they share a life with the saints of all ages and places? This last point is made clear by the tradition of "patron" saints, of giving saints' names to children, and of the presence of the saints' icons in the home.

The Church's rites can be carried into the home and must be if the family is to be, in fact, the "little Church." Children can be encouraged to set up icon centers in their home as places of prayer, and to engage in daily Bible readings, and prayer at meals and on such other occasions as before a family trip. Family traditions, not uncommon among those of ethnic origins, should be adopted for holidays such as Christmas, Pascha, the Dormition, etc. The parish can help parents establish such traditional symbols as the advent wreath or create entirely new traditions.

The people of the Church must share the prayer of the Church. Do they know the basic formal prayers of the Church? Do they share it with other members of the family? Keep in mind that children do not have to understand the prayers. Understanding is quite secondary, they must learn, as we all must, that the prayers we pray are the prayers of the Church which have been used for thousands of years and which are now prayed by millions of fellow Christians around the world. This is why formal prayer is so central: it both establishes and feeds a sense of community.

The Church is not static; it is also service. The Church is not simply the reality of God's presence here. It is God's active presence and it must be open to the needs of the world—to feeding and caring for the world—in the tradition of Christian hospitality. Are all members of the Church given an opportunity to serve and care for the world? Does the local Church plan and encourage caring programs? Does it care for its own people, its shut-ins, its disabled, its hospitalized? If the Church closes in on itself, it ceases to be the Church and becomes a club, albeit with inspiring ideas, but not alive to its Lord, who calls it to love in word and in deed.

Finally, parallel to this, and as significant, is the social aspect of the local Church by which community is both created and enhanced. All of us need structures to support us and a group of people to share our beliefs, our history, and our symbols. These are essential to healthy spiritual and emotional development. Parish events—dances, skating parties, picnics—all enhance and validate the individual's belief structure. Many parishes have multi-generational social activities—dinners, plays, fairs, picnics. But all ages must be given some responsibility. Being part of a community is having responsibility for that community. Responsibility in turn creates a sense of belonging.

The second foundation I considered was that of the family as the formative agency or the primary educator of its members. The family does not exist only for its children any more than education is only for childhood. A systems approach enables us to consider the family from a variety of "real" perspectives and to see it as a source of pre-theological characteristics basic to the development and continued growth of the faith life of the family members.

But while the family is the single most significant agency of learning, it is the agency over which the Church has the least control. The family tends to be a private agency and permits little external interference except from specialists (but even they posses limited access). The Church can approach the family from two perspectives, which can be distinguished more logically than practically, First, the Church can encourage Christian family life by focusing on the family's ministry to its own members, creating the atmosphere/disposition for healthy and mature Christian faith lives to develop. The parish can intercede as the agency that enables the family to enhance its ministry to its members through parent- or family-centered programs dealing with topics such as communication in the home, disciplining children at different ages, age-related child characteristics, the role of the father in the emotional development of the child, and so on. The parish can also offer itself as the clearing house for family support specialists whose services whether financial, emotional, psychological, or educational are frequently useful to families in cultures of rapid social change. The parish can and should invite specialists to offer workshops that the parish priest or the parents think are needed. Certainly, one of the most therapeutic devices available to parents is simply talking with other parents of children of the same age. This would be, for instance, a valuable opportunity for parents of teenagers to discuss the relationship with their teens or to deal with a topic such as sexuality, which while it enables the family to minister to its own members, also gives them an opportunity to discuss the traditional teaching of the Scripture and Church on questions related to ethics.

Second, a family-centered ministry should focus on the ministry of the Church to the family itself. The Church's job is to teach the family about the life of the Church and what the Church teaches about the role of the family; these programs can seek to enhance the spiritual life of the members of the family as family and as individuals. A logical starting point would focus on how the family treats the child's Church school work and what the family can do to reinforce it at home. For instance, how can parents use contemporary secular literature to illustrate Christian moral or theological themes. The Orthodox Christian Education Commission recommends several dozen books available from any good public library for use with its own curriculum at home by parents.[4] Having a librarian display and discuss these books would promote/enhance/support the ministry of the Church to the family and, in turn, the ministry of the fmaily to its members.

The Church must also encourage celebration in the home. Celebration belongs in the Christian home because it is the place where children first come to trust the world as essentially good, reliable, and exciting. Celebrating Church festivals, secular holidays, personal events, even the first fruits of the family's garden can and should be part of every Orthodox home, and the Church, if it cannot provide the details, should provide the skills for parents to create such celebration in the home. The parent or family meetings can deal with icons, prayers, rituals, and the family as the server of the needs of others. A new and valuable approach for family-centered ministry is the so-called "Family Clustering" model developed by Margaret Sawin,[5] which seeks to bring together family members for simultaneous intergenerational learning activities. Short of this the parish can and should make use of any intergenerational activity, in which the members of the family can work together on a common theme (e.g., creation, the world, ecology), or work separately discussing, each on his own level, the meaning of the theme selected. The family is the essential educator which at the same time fits into the socialization model developed earlier. The Church must focus on a two-fold approach: (1) ministry of the family to its members, and (2) ministry of the Church to the family.

Finally, in considering the third foundation—the developing person—I have shown how this idea of the human person as *developing* is central to growing to moral maturity through the agency of the tri-polar influence of behavioral (social), psychoanalytical, and developmental factors in a person's life. The age/stage of a person is critical to (1) the content of what we teach and (2) the methods we select to teach the child. The needs, interests, abilities of the learners condition what goes on in the educational enterprise.

It is important to understand that from both a pedagogical and theological perspective any particular aspect of the Church can be related, apprehended, and presented in a wide variety of ways suited to the developmental needs, interests, and abilities of the learners. This can be done without betraying the faith of the Church. Any aspect of the life of the Church is an appropriate means of teaching about the entire life of the Church. We need only recall the variety of explanations of Christ's redemptive work throughout the history of Christian thought; similarly, the concepts of original sin, personal sin, the Eucharist, and creation can be communicated on a variety of levels and perspectives (e.g., factual, conceptual, and personal). The level and approach must be appropriate to the age, needs, interests, and abilities of the learners. This determination will by the sheer force of the decision determine how we teach it, what method we select to enable the information to speak to the learner. No meaningful learning or teaching can take place without considering the personhood of the learner, but few, if any, of our contemporary Orthodox education programs take into account assumptions about the role of the learner, the role of the teacher, and the role of the community. They are heavily content-centered.

Having affirmed the centrality of the nature of the personhood and persons, then parents, priests, and teachers must emphasize those methods and materials that are suited to the age/stage of the person as well as the nature of Christian personhood. We must affirm that our teaching and our expectation must be congruent with the needs, interests, and abilities of the learners; for instance, we must teach with the understanding, as outlined in chapter four, that the more conceptual approach and material is appropriate to the older learner, especially those in their teenage years.

We must also use methods that take seriously the nature of Christian personhood. This means realizing, for instance, that genuine communication in which messages are exchanged, and listening and speaking take place, is essential to any learning situation and is rooted in the respect that personhood commands. Every person has value in himself, and this value demands that he be part of the learning process, that he be made responsible for sharing in his own growth. The patristic notion of personhood demands that the learner be active in the process of his own creation, of his own development. For too long we in the Orthodox Church have accepted methods that place the burden for learning on the teacher. We also have a responsibility to teach people how to teach themselves. No method is tolerable as a teaching method that does not involve the learner in the process of learning since learning is process and not product oriented. This is, of course, especially true of the kind of learning that involves communicating meaning. Christian learning is meaning-filled learning that must *become* part of the learner. The lecture approach, except with a highly motivated group, for instance, is convenient, easy, universal, and almost useless as an educating tool. Even when useful, however, it is estimated that people recall only ten percent of what they hear in a lecture and slightly more of what they read. You cannot give people meaning; you can help them to discover meaning. Other techniques characterize effective teaching and at the same time take account of the Christian notion of personhood—the use of silence in an educational setting, the skill of phrasing and directing effective questions, guiding a discussion, organizing a concept, and so on—all speak to a meaningful learning atmosphere.

If, as I have said, the person and the nature of Christian personhood are taken seriously, then we must also respect "where" people are, what they need, and what part of the Gospel they need to hear. I contend that we do not have to teach eveything there is to know about the Church to be faithful to the Church; however, we do have to teach those aspects of Church life that are typical of the entire content of the Church.

C. Ellis Nelson has noted that education is a particularly human process that should not be identified with the work of the Spirit. Unfortunately, on a practical level, much sloppy planning, programming, and teaching is taking place with ill-defined goals, poorly stated objectives, and inadequate materials because all too many people believe that the Holy Spirit is ultimately responsible for the teaching enterprise. We must never be forced to choose between the work of the Spirit and education.[5]

Unfortunately, all too many, if not all of our Christian education programs are rooted in the fear of not doing anything. This fear can be overcome by working founda-tions—Church, family, person—that give us a perspective from which to operate and plan for the future we want. The Orthodox Church in North America has the opportunity to base its educational enterprise on firm foundations which are at once rooted in the Church and rooted in the best of contemporary pedagogical research. Christian education rests on a series of theoretical and practical foundations, on a series of assumptions about the Church, the family, the person, and their respective roles in the total education of the parish community.

Chapter 5 Footnotes

[1]Gloria Durka, "Modeling Religious Education for the Future," in James M. Lee, (ed.), *The Religious Education We Need* (Mishawaka, IN: Religious Education Press, 1977), 103.

[2]Gloria Durka, "Preparing for the Professions," in Maria Harris, (ed.), *Parish Religious Education* (New York: Paulist Press, 1978), 169-187, at 173.

[3]See J.L. Boojamra, *Creative Activities I* (Englewood, NJ: Department of Christian Education, 1975), *passim*.

[4]C. Ellis Nelson, "Is Church Education Something Special?" *Religious Education* 67 (January-February, 1972), 7.

[5]John H. Westerhoff, "The Visionary: Planning for the Future," in *A Colloquy on Christian Education* (Philadelphia: A Pilgrim Press Book, 1972), 236-247.

Selected Bibliography

Allport, Gordon. *The Nature of Prejudice*. Reading, MA: Addison-Wesley, 1954.

Apostolos-Cappadonam, Diane. *The Sacred Play of Children*. New York: Seabury Press, 1983.

Barber, Lucie. *Teaching Christian Values*. Birmingham, AL: Religious Education Press, 1984.

Bellah, Robert, et al. *Habits of the Heat*. New York: Harper and Row, 1986.

Berger, Peter. *A Rumor of Angels*. Garden City: Doubleday, 1970.

Boojamra, John. "Socialization as a Historical Model for Christian Integration," *St. Vladimir's Theological Quarterly*, 25 (1981), 219-237.

Boojamra, John. "Theological and Pedagogical Perspectives on the Family as Educator," *Greek Orthodox Theological Review,* 29 (1984), 1-33.

Chirban, John T. *Human Growth and Faith*. Washington, D.C.: University Press of America, 1981.

Curran, Dolores. *Who, Me Teach My Child Religion?* Minneapolis: Winston Press, 1974.

Dobson, James. *Dare to Discipline*. New York: Bantam Books, 1978.

Dreikurs, Rudolf. *Children the Challenge*. New York: Hawthorn/Dutton, 1964.

Durka, Gloria and Joanmarie Smith. *Family Ministry*. Minneapolis: Winston Press, 1980.

Duska, Ronald, and Mariellen Whelan. *Moral Development: A Guide to Piaget and Kohlberg.* New York: Paulist Press, 1965.

Elkind, David. *All Grown Up and No Place to Go.* Reading, MA: Addison-Wesley, 1984.

Elkind, David. *The Hurried Child.* Reading, MA: Addison-Wesley, 1981.

Erikson, Erik. *Identity: Youth and Crisis.* New York: Norton, 1968.

Forell, George W. *History of Christian Ethics.* Vol 1. Minneapolis: Augsburg, 1979.

Fraiberg, Selma. *The Magic Years.* New York: Charles Scribner's Sons, 1959.

Galbraith, Ronald, and Thomas Jones. *Moral Reasoning: A Teaching Handbook for Adapting Kohlberg to the Classroom.* Minneapolis: Greenhaven Press, 1976.

Goldman, Ronald. *Religious Thinking From Childhood to Adolescence.* New York: The Seabury Press, 1964.

Kelsey, Morton. *Can Christians be Educated?* Mishawaka, IN: Religious Education Press, 1977.

Kohlberg, Lawrence. "Stages of Moral Development as a Basis for Moral Education,": in *Moral Education Interdisciplinary Approach.* New York: Newman Press, 1970, 86-88.

Koulomzin, Sophie. *Our Church and Our Children.* Crestwood, NY: St. Vladimir's Seminary Press, 1975.

Kenison, Kenneth, and the Carnegie Council on Children. *All Our Children: The American Family Under Pressure.* New York: Harcourt, Brace, Jovanovich, 1978.

Lauer, Eugene, and John Mlecko. *A Christian Understanding of the Human Person.* New York: Paulist Press, (1982).

178

McDannell, Colleen. *The Christian Home in Victorian America*, 1840-1900. Bloomington, IN: Indiana University Press, 1986.

Macpherson, Michael C. *The Family Years*. Minneapolis: Winston Press, 1981.

Osborn, Eric. *Ethical Patterns in Early Christian Thought*. Cambridge: University Press, 1978.

Sawin, Margaret. *Family Enrichment with Family Clusters*. Valley Forge: Judson Press, 1979.

Schwebel, Milton and Jane Ralph. *Piaget in the Classroom*. New York: Basic Books, 1973.

Strommen, Merton. *Five Cries of Youth*. San Francisco: Harper and Row, 1979.

Westerhoff, John H. *Bringing Up Children in the Christian Faith*. Minneapolis: Winston Press, 1980.

Westerhoff, John H. *Will Our Children Have Faith?* New York: Seabury Press, 1976.

Winn, Marie. *Children without Childhood*. New York: Pantheon, 1983.

Index